'Steve Clarke is the business
presenter with no fluffy fairy s
seminars and conferences ar
speakers and I rate Steve amongst
He delivered his message in a very practical, precise and simple way. Great humour, engaging and empowering. Thanks Steve. You rock!'

Mark Tracey - Love2print Clothing

'He gave a really great speech. Engaging and witty and left the audience feeling very positive. What he said made absolute sense and I think we have all benefited from his knowledge and experience.'

Tonya Meers - Little Creative Days Ltd

'No complaining! Steve gave a great presentation yesterday. Steve's delivery and ideas came at just the right time and over the coming weeks I plan to take action as a direct result and change some poor sales habits.'

Ashley Marshall - Jumpworks

'His presentation was completely inspiring and thoroughly enjoyable. His explanation of the 3 sales teams within a business is certainly worth listening to and I would certainly recommend that if you have the chance to hear Steve speak you get along to one of his events. Thanks for all your help and wisdom!'

Nathan Lomax - Early Entrepreneurs

'Steve is a brilliant speaker and uses humour very effectively to communicate his message. He certainly made me think and re-evaluate how I approach sales. If you get the opportunity to see Steve speak make sure you take it.'

Elaine Carr - Marketing Consultant

'Steve gave a great keynote speech, thoroughly entertaining with some clear takeaway messages which will help everyone in the room!'

Gary Burns - Potential3 Ltd

'Steve is a highly engaging speaker who presents with authority and verve. He is also an advocate of SALES as a professional occupation and whilst everyone will benefit from hearing him speak, those who look down on sales as a dirty if necessary, thing may even benefit most!'

Christopher Marrum - Marrum Distribution Ltd

'He had a powerful message which he delivered with humour and great confidence. An engaging talk with tons of relevant content. BE WARNED - only listen to Steve if you want to be inspired to take your business to greater success!'

Karen Haynes - Professional Property Investor

Eureka Moments:

Business and personal success ... made simple

Steve Clarke

3P PUBLISHING

Eureka Moments:
Business and personal success…
made simple

First published in 2016 in the UK
This reprint 2020

3P Publishing
C E C, London Road
Corby, NN17 5EU

A catalogue number for this book is available from the British Library

ISBN 978-1-911559-18-4

This book is dedicated to my gorgeous wife Susanne, our five children and our growing tribe of grandchildren.
Each day, in their own special ways, they remind me of the meaning of success.
For me...success, happiness and peace of mind come from knowing I've made the best effort to be the best version of me that I'm capable of being.
Success comes from a combination of the right attitude and action – simple.

Content

EUREKA MOMENTS

Foreword

I'd seen Steve working with a Hertfordshire Business Forum and again at the Professional Speaker Association Conference in London. I jumped at the chance of asking him to support the work I do with Make it Happen (a seminar for owner operators of SME businesses and middle managers of large corporates) and iTANG which is a charity designed to support young people who are out of work develop the right attitude to gain meaningful employment. I knew they would all benefit from his experience and attitude.

Why did I engage Steve? He is easy to work with, has his ego in check and wants to understand the brief so that he can deliver excellent results for the target audience. Once on the platform, he is engaging and insightful giving practical advice and examples of how to get to a 'yes'. He has a wonderful mixture of monologue and dialogue as he relates stories, analogies, and experiences to the delegates so as to tease out their thinking, and action. His latest book *Eureka Moments* does this perfectly in print too.

I'm very happy to recommend Steve as a professional speaker and presenter on all matters related to sales psychology or business performance. Thanks Steve for your support - keep doing what you do to help others.

I hope you enjoy the book and apply all that Steve has to share.

Kriss Akabusi MBE

Chief Energizing Officer - Manifesting Magical Moments

Introduction

***'Formal education will make you a good living. Self-education will make you a fortune.'* Jim Rohn**

Congratulations on investing in yourself and thank you for reading my book.

I've stripped out any Harvard University thought leadership and MBA gobbledegook and just kept it plain and simple, highly effective content that works. It's really the only way I know.

Each letter of the *EUREKA* acronym forms the various chapter headings. They will help you reflect on your own life, your relationships, your job or your own business and consider how you approach things and whether you are living your life on purpose and enjoying the benefits of 'yes' culture.

When the simplicity of increasing your opportunities for getting to a 'yes' falls into focus and you apply daily planned activity that you take from this book, positive results will follow. The more you discover the joy of getting to a 'yes', the more ingrained it becomes. You will very soon realise you have the ability to create and pass on a 'yes' culture to others.

My hope is that within the pages of this book will be a number of light bulb moments. The moment when you 'get it,' that will help you move forwards, help you move towards your goals. Your *Eureka* moments if you will.

When you have one of those *Eureka* moments capture it. Use a highlighter, write on the pages, create your own summary along with the summary at the end of each chapter, I don't mind, just capture it then, most importantly, act on it.

Some thoughts may result in an idea you want to action, they may be something you'll decide to abandon.

eureka |ˌjʊ(ə)ˈriːkə|

exclamation

a cry of joy or satisfaction when one finds or discovers something. *The answer hit me. 'Eureka!' I cried.*

Here's a *Eureka* moment to kick things off. Beliefs and mindset shape our behaviour, this in turn will determine our actions, these actions or inactions produce an outcome - our results.

Change your mindset and all will be fine and dandy. That's it. Close the book you're done, if it were just that simple. Let me take you back to when the lights came on for me - one of my first *Eureka* moments that was to shape my entire life.

.....

If you want to see a change, it's down to you.

Whoever decided education should culminate in exams at the same time as your male hormones are raging needs a serious talking to.

I didn't do too well at school in terms of exams, but was an 'A' student in terms of flirting with the opposite sex. It was girls over studying and exams any time for me.

Whilst I was smart enough, I wasn't an academic. I didn't find the company of the clever crowd stimulating or fun. I hung out with the wrong people, the bad boys. I never did anything particularly naughty, no drugs or real trouble. Looking back, it was a very early lesson to watch out for the company you keep; they have the ability to lift you up or drag you down.

The result? I left school at sixteen with no purpose or direction in my life and no real qualifications to my name. I learned some interesting lessons, but none that would help in the workplace!

By the age of 18 I'd had various jobs including the tea boy in a cafe, stacking shelves in a pub, a cardboard box designer (tougher than it sounds), becoming a trainee manager at a gents outfitters in Golders Green and eventually reaching the lofty heights of petrol pump attendant.

Recently I was reminded how times have changed, and how old I really am, when I told this story to an audience at the University of Surrey in Guildford. There was an awkward tumbleweed moment when I realised the students were too young to even know what a petrol pump attendant even was!

If you are also of an age where this means nothing to you: My job was to stand on the forecourt of the petrol station in all weathers getting cold and often wet and pump fuel into other people's cars for them.

The forecourt encounter that changed my life

If you could have been with me on that dark, wet, stormy winter evening in December 1977, you would have witnessed one simple act that was to change my life forever.

As I stood alone and cold facing the elements, my next customer drew up to the pump.

It was a very smart, brand new car (smart for the times folks - go and Google it, metallic brown, 1600cc Ford Cortina MK IV). I was in awe of this beautiful shiny beast as it pulled to a halt alongside me.

Someday, I thought, someday I'll have one of those... someday.

(Many years later I was to read a great book by Brian Tracy in which he describes the place called 'Someday Isle', meaning the place people dream of and yet will never get to which in fact is written - someday I'll... as opposed to Isle - because if all you do is dream with thoughts like that, someday, you won't).

The driver wound the window down just a few inches, he was no mug, he wasn't coming out in the rain. He called out from the tiny opening in the window from the warmth of his sumptuous interior.

"Fill her up mate."

And straight back up with the window.

To my amazement, then disappointment, almost envy, I realised in an instant that the guy in the smart, new, warm car had to be near enough the same age as me.

This felt so desperately unfair.

How could this be? I wasn't a bad person; I wasn't an idiot. I might have preferred girls to exams, but was this really how I should be made to feel for making that choice at the time. It sucked!

What on earth did he do for a living that provided such a car I wondered as I continued to fill his tank and the rain continued to dribble down the neck of my greasy overalls?

As he passed me payment through the 'just open' window I commented, "Lovely car mate. How come you get to drive around in this beauty and I'm standing out here in the rain? Still that's just how things go, I suppose," I said.

"That's what I used to think too," he replied.

Then he passed me a cassette tape. (Ok young ones, Google that as well if you have to!)

"Take a listen to this, it changed my life. It could do the same for you."

And off he drove, with a beautiful rasp from the exhaust that rang in my ears as he shifted gear and disappeared into the night.

'Arrogant prat,' I thought. Still, my day was nearly over.

Once home, as I undressed that night and got ready to soak in a warming bath in an attempt to regain my circulation, the cassette he'd given to me fell to the floor from my pocket.

In my bedroom, I clicked the eject button on my Philips tape recorder, purchased specifically because it had one of those ultra-slow motion, very sexy, ejects. Remember the ones? Hit the button and for a full 10 seconds the lid slowly opened to receive the tape - no? Just me then?

Anyway, I slid the tape in, pressed play and laid back on the bed as I'd defrosted. I don't know quite what I was expecting. Just some funky music I think really.

Instead it was my first exposure to any kind of personal development material.

Up piped the strangest voice I'd ever heard! It was that of Hilary Hinton Ziglar, better known to millions around the world as the late, great Zig Ziglar from the USA's Deep South - Alabama.

Straaaaaaange voice, but compelling.

The tape I recall was called *See you at the top* or something very similar. I was totally mesmerised. I listened to the entire tape and drifted off into a deep sleep feeling invisible.

This was positive stuff, the like of which I'd never encountered. Why did nobody teach this stuff at school I wondered and still wonder for that matter.

The essence of Zig's message was that **if you want to see a change in your fortunes it's down to you** and nobody else to bring about that change.

I don't know who that guy in the Cortina was, but I thank him from the bottom of my heart. He changed my life forever with the small gesture of sharing that tape.

I encourage every one of you to take responsibility for your future - don't wait for others to change - it's down to you and it's all about your attitude and the actions you take!

Do you have to just accept your lot? No. Can you change the direction your life is heading? Yes, you can.

There's a ton of great self-development material out there. You may even be one of thousands of people that buy the books, give them a cursory glance and then up it goes on the shelf with all the others.

That's not self-development, that's shelf development and it won't help you at all.

"Attitude makes the difference." Zig Ziglar

Chapter 1

Find a way, don't find an excuse!

'There are some four million different kinds of animals and plants in the world. Four million different solutions to the problem of staying alive.' David Attenborough

It's a new day. Don't be afraid, be enthusiastic and focused. Just imagine what you can achieve today if you put your mind to it and take action.

What happened yesterday is done. Let's start over.

Focus on what you want to achieve and why? Who can you help and how? Then make it so. Don't let anything or anyone hold you back. Enthusiasm and action trumps the lot. Be focused and get at it!
How do you view the world? Are you a glass half full or a glass half empty kind of a person?

Attitude and mindset play a huge part in helping us achieve our goals. Let's try a simple test. What do you see when you read this?

Opportunityisnowhere

Opportunity is 'nowhere' or opportunity is 'now here!' Show the same thing to a seven year old and they see…
'Opportunity snow's here!!' Got to love their enthusiasm.

Opportunities are all around us, we just need to be able to identify them and seize them. We need to be able to find a way and not find an excuse. The problem is that often an excuse is easier to make than the effort required to maximise any given opportunity.

I've spent years studying successful people, successful businesses, successful sports men, women and teams. How do they think, how do they act, what do they do?

Great news - **Success leaves clues.**

For more than 10 years my good friend Warren Cass, the founder of one of the UK's leading business support membership groups, *Business Scene*, has made an annual pilgrimage to the slopes and he doesn't like to ski alone; so he set up 'Netski'.

He thought it would be a great idea to invite like-minded business people and entrepreneurs to spend time together on and off the *piste*. The idea being, you get to make new friends and hang out with old ones. Share thoughts, ideas and stories and enjoy the fresh mountain air together. Inspired thinking all round.

What an opportunity to mix with and learn from smart people, I thought.

Like many, I love the all round alpine experience. Fresh air, breathtaking views, exercise and of course the *apres ski*, (the highlight for many, Warren included as he demonstrated... repeatedly). So I decided to 'find a way not find an excuse' and joined the group.

I very quickly realised I was privileged to be in the company of some amazing and very interesting people. The group has, (pardon the pun) snowballed. There were 60 of us on this particular trip! Over the course of the week I got into some fascinating conversations with people from a broad spectrum of industries and from all over the country.

Energised and fascinated by the collective brain power, during conversations I made a point of eliciting what motivates and drives them on. Was there a 'yes' culture at play? What were the secrets to the success of this amazing group I found myself in? It was no surprise that many patterns repeated; 'yes' success leaves clues.

So collated from various conversations I had over the week are the **Seven Secrets to Success from Skiers off the Slopes, (**none of which are about "bending zeee knees").

1. Knowledge isn't power – it's the application of knowledge that counts.

Yes, there was an obvious thirst for knowledge. They never stop learning. They read, they ask questions and (on the whole) they listen well. The difference is that they then take action, as in massive action. If knowledge alone was power the world would be run by librarians. It's the application that counts.

2. Don't worry about asking for advice.

Many of those I spoke to, despite being at the top of their field and top of their game told me that they had coaches and mentors they would turn to when they wanted advice or to talk over challenges. Whilst they could make great and tough decisions, they didn't go it alone.

3. It's important to become a great leader.

Yes, delegation, inspiration and motivation were key messages. In order to grow and scale you can't do everything. You have to act and think more strategically. There was a clear message about becoming a strong leader. People follow great leaders. If people aren't following you, you're not a leader, you're just going for a walk.

4. Get out of your comfort zone.

The most successful people I spoke with all operate at their best when they're stretched, not resting in their comfort zone. It was clear that in order to achieve the success that others only dream of you must push beyond where you're comfortable into your stretch zone, sometimes on the edge of panic. Yes, they all get comfortable feeling uncomfortable and push on.

5. Don't live in the past.

My friend, double Olympic medalist, Kriss Akabusi, says 'the past is for reference, not for residence.' And yes, this came out in several discussions too. Learn from the past, don't go back, don't dwell on things; drive forwards, onwards and upwards. Acknowledge when things go wrong, don't dwell on it, learn from it. Change what you can, accept what you can't, let go. Move on. When things go well, celebrate. Don't stop there, push on.

6. Surround yourself with positive people.

Yes, *Netski* delivered on this brilliantly. Life is too short to hang out with small minded moaners, they will drag you down. If you find yourself in the company of negative people; don't just walk away from them… RUN!

7. **WTF**

A favourite of mine – Where's The Focus? Yes, the highly successful people I spoke with were all laser focused on where they were going and why. Where's your focus?

What a great trip it was: I decided straight away, I needed to find a way to go again the next year and not find an excuse not to so I've paid my deposit, I'm already signed up and booked on to the next one.

.....

We're all in sales - get over it.

Before we get into the *Eureka* acronym that forms each of the following chapters of this book I need to get your agreement on one thing - it's this:

It's my firm belief that whatever else we may be in life… we're all in sales.

In its simplest form, selling is essentially about getting to 'yes'. Agreed? 'Yes?' Well that's a good start. Creating a 'yes' culture throughout your business and in all areas of your life can deliver consistent and positive results.

In business, often one of the first big hurdles I need to help people overcome, is to face the fact that irrespective of the title on their business card - they're in sales. The CEO, CFO, MD, receptionist or delivery driver, they all have a role to play in sales today.

When I ask people what do they do or what business are they in? They'll tell me I'm a solicitor, I'm a hairdresser, I'm in marketing and so on.

Wrong! We're all in sales! Get over it.

Selling today is not all about closing a deal on a second hand car. *Eureka* selling is ethical selling, helping people solve problems and creating a win-win scenario, that's sales made simple.

The world has changed and we're not going back. Selling is no longer someone's job within an organisation - it's everyone's job.

A child asks why, how and when until they get to 'yes'. It's what any good sales person does too.

A teacher has to sell her class the idea of chemistry or maths as an engaging topic to get buy in from her pupils in order for them to get the results they want in later life. She's in sales.

A doctor has to sell you the belief in his ability to prescribe the best remedy for your ailment and restore good health. He's in sales.

The *Eureka Selling Methodology* helps large companies, entrepreneurial business owners and sales teams win more business. It will also help you get to 'yes' more often with internal stakeholders, work colleagues and external clients. It will even help you get to 'yes' with friends and family too.

Whatever job you have, whatever role you think you play - you're almost certainly in sales in some way, shape or form.

Let's be clear, **this book is not a sales manual** full of manipulative closing tricks and strategies to win more business. Thank goodness, the days of the ABC (Always Be Closing) of sales are way behind us.

For those in sales (and we need to agree soon that that's pretty much all of us) cold calling is dead and traditional advertising doesn't work.

Most will breathe a sigh of relief to the first point and may be puzzled by the second, don't panic, I will explain fully as we work through the book.

Before we move on, let's take one problem head on - it's one of mindset. Think of all the words you would use to describe the typical attributes associated with a 'salesman' or 'saleswoman.' Be honest, don't hold back, what are the adjectives you'd use?

List them here, come on, what picture do you have in your mind when you think - salesman?

OK , if I were to be reading your mind, these would be the kind of words I believe you'd come up with and the images of the typical salesman you might have in mind.

Negative	Positive
slippery	hard working
slimy	focused
sleazy	persistent
cocky	positive
greedy	goal driven
pressure	helpful
money grabbers	resilient
dishonest	good listeners
gift of the gab	passionate
untrustworthy	reliable
pushy	problem solver
insincere	friendly
selfish	knowledgeable
aggressive	
manipulative	
arrogant	
liar	

The list goes on - right?

I have run this exercise with thousands of people at different events around the world and the same words are repeated, irrespective of the geography or the industry that I might be talking to.

I've grouped the words here into their negative or positive connotations. Rather ironically, even if I'm speaking with people who accept they're 'in sales', there will still be an imbalance of negative to positive word associations with being in sales.

With that kind of image in mind is it any wonder people push back at the thought of being ‘in sales?’ You don’t want to be thought of in that way I’m sure. I most certainly don’t.

Well, don’t worry. The world has changed and we’re not going back. Those kind of sales people used to exist, they still do in one or two industries, but rest assured, they are fast becoming extinct.

There’s a Latin phrase used in some legal contracts, you may be familiar with the term: *caveat emptor*. It means ‘buyer beware.’ This should be replaced today with *caveat venditor*, which means ‘seller beware.’

The world has changed and we’re not going back.

Anybody trying to squeeze people into an unfair contract or an over-priced product and the world will know about it in a nanosecond thanks to the highly connected world we live in today and the reach of social media.

A few years ago I delivered a keynote speech at a conference for the governing body for many of the world’s leading timeshare operators. Ethical selling was central to my talk and it featured in a workshop I ran for them too.

This year I was asked by the same governing body to travel to Tenerife to shoot a series of short videos about ‘ethical selling’ for them. When I mention timeshare, many of you will roll your eyes and form a mental image of a timeshare salesman. Correct?

He's probably described perfectly by many of the negative words in the left hand column. Correct again?

I found it ironic when speaking at a conference for one of our countries top banks that they also laughed at the idea of ethical selling and timeshare being used in the same sentence...

"Whoa, hold on a moment, was it mis-selling of timeshare that created the global economic crisis?" I asked. Some rather embarrassed looks and raised eyebrows said it all.

This year, I'm back speaking at their time share conference again as they are serious about changing their image and their culture. They want to get more people to 'yes' in an ethical fashion; they realised the only way to sell today is through ethical selling.

They also know, because I've explained it to them, every business today has three distinct sales teams irrespective of whether they are a small start up or multinational giant.

If you're reading this book, but you're not in business for yourself the three teams concept still applies to you too.

Remember, sales is no longer exclusively 'someone's' job within a business. It's fast becoming everybody's job.

Buyers are now more informed than ever before. All the technical information, research, reviews and recommendations are available to them at the touch of a button. Moreover, the answers they are seeking are often available right in the palm of their hands thanks to smart phones and tablets.

No longer does the old school salesman or saleswoman have the upper hand in terms of information and knowledge. Gone are the old days of the old ABC of sales… Always Be Closing, and that's a good thing!

We have moved from a world of *caveat emptor* (buyer beware) to one of *caveat venditor* (seller beware). Not only does the customer have information available to them, but they have the means to communicate both good and bad experiences with the world in a heart beat.

People today, want a fair deal from people they **know, like and trust.** Getting people to exchange what they have for something we have is a very natural occurrence. To sell today is to serve. To sell more – serve better, simple.

Today, to see an increase in sales, to get to 'yes' more often, we must improve all round communication. All staff that have any contact with customers, in any business, no matter how remote, should learn the new ABC of sales – **Always Be Caring.**

Every business as I see it, now has three distinct sales teams:

The Regular, The Reluctant and The Referral

For your business to 'thrive, not just survive', (the title of my previous book, explaining the proven formula for business success), you must have a strategy and tactical plan for each of these very different 'sales teams'.

The Regular Sales Team:

This would be considered our traditional sales force. It may involve retail staff, perhaps business development consultants or telesales people. You get the idea, the more traditional roles.

It's funny, until recently I felt that people were more often than not hiding behind the title of business development because they didn't like the idea of being seen as a sales person as previously described. And that may actually be the case.

However, I now believe the term 'business development' more aptly describes the role of the traditional sales person today. For sales to soar - it's all about developing strong, genuine relationships. We should, perhaps, think about banishing the idea of 'closing a sale' and switch it to 'opening a relationship'. Which one sounds more positive and mutually beneficial to you?

For the record, I don't believe we work in either the B2B or B2C space any more, (business to business or business to consumer). For sales to skyrocket try thinking about P2P instead: people to people.

I have found more and more that clients can soon become friends and friends can equally become clients. The two worlds have merged into one; this is due, mainly, to the proliferation of social media.

I used to have an issue with this. For ages I tried to swim against the tide. I'd have my personal Facebook page and my business Facebook page and never the twain should meet… or so I thought. But what I've increasingly found is that people want to get to know the people they are engaging with.

If you connect with me on Facebook, you'll not see pictures of me in my Speedos, trust me – you wouldn't want to see that! You'll not be privy to some elements of my private life as some things should remain private and sacrosanct. However, you will see pictures of me walking Trevor, my dog. You'll see me enjoying family time. You'll see results of my run or my bike ride. You will get to know me as a person. I really enjoy doing business with people I know, like and trust. Facebook is one platform that has allowed us to get to know people behind the business facade.

Just heed the warning; if you are portraying a business image of sweetness and light, but living life on Facebook as a foul mouthed bricklayer with full blown Tourette's there will be no hiding the mismatch. This lack of congruency can, and will, cost you business. This fundamental error has cost people their job and prevented some people from landing the one they really wanted. Think before you post.

It used to be true that what goes on tour stays on tour. Now, what goes on tour, goes straight onto Facebook. Post with care, but remain true to you.

Traditional sales teams or business development teams may have traded their rolodex for a CRM system and their brief case for a smart phone, but ostensibly their role remains that of the farmer. Sew the seeds, nurture the crop and reap the rewards.

Sales teams who start to find it tough to compete and win business often point straight to pricing or fierce competition which is rubbish. They need to learn how to connect and engage with people at an emotional level. Very few people just buy on price. We are price sensitive, sure, but it's just one factor.

When you build strong relationships and deliver outstanding service that's how you can ring fence your customers.

Do you know what a 'Boma' is?

A 'Boma' is the name given to an enclosure built principally from sticks to protect an african tribes livestock from predators. Quite literally a 'ring fence' to protect the things that are most valuable to them from outside dangers.

As I stood within the relative safety of our camp's boma, whilst on safari in South Africa, waiting for our ranger to take us back out for our evening safari adventure, I got to thinking.

How do we 'ring fence' our customers today?
I remember times when businesses used to tie clients into lengthy contracts and felt they were safe as they had ink on paper, signed contracts.

They would even include onerous break clauses which would inflict the client with financial penalties and inconvenience should they wish to change suppliers in the hope they'd remain loyal.

It sounds crazy and hard to believe, but I promise you it used to be so. Not any more. The world has changed.

The only way you can truly ‘ring fence’ your clients today is to build strong, long lasting relationships based on mutual trust. Consider their needs before your own and deliver consistent, outstanding customer service.

When you have a strong relationship you could dismantle your boma and your clients would not stray. Take down your boma and the predators would not be able to get to your precious livestock.

When we returned to our camp after dark our boma looked safe, warm and welcoming too. Camp fires lit, we enjoyed an incredible barbecue in safety under the glorious night skies. We were happy to be home.

That’s how you want your clients feeling too. They’re home, they’re safe and well looked after and that way you’ll ring fence your clients from the competition.

Build your boma.

The Reluctant Sales Team:

In this group we have anyone that has even the slightest contact with clients or prospects including the finance team, admin staff or I.T support, these people are very much in sales today, they probably don’t realise it, but they can have a huge influence over sales, or worse the lack of sales! I know many a finance team who act like the sales prevention team!

People buy from people they know, like and trust. This group of people need to recognise that being in ‘sales’ is not a dirty word. It's not all those words you've used to describe the archetypical sales person.

If we believe that our company, products and services are great would we suggest our own mum buys from us? Of course, you'd make a strong case and recommend the best thing for her, right?

Again, this needs to be explained, taught and practiced, but the impact can be immense, more on this in a moment.

The Referral Sales Team:

This is made up from your happy clients. These happy clients will give referrals and recommendations. These can come in the form of written testimonials, video clips, posts on social media... the list is almost endless, but it's incredibly powerful, when worked with a strategy. (Again more of this when we cover the chapter on Engagement.)

.....

So when I asked you to write down your list of words to describe someone in 'sales' I said this was the problem - one of mindset, how you think of that archetypal sales person you don't want to be and how this affects the results you're seeing in your business, your job or your personal life.

It works at a subconscious level.

Picture this: You have an apple tree, but you're tired of apples. You don't like the result the tree is producing i.e. apples. You fancy a change. You pick all the apples from the tree and say come on tree, grow me some oranges. With all the positive energy you can muster, you think come on tree, give me some oranges. What do you get when the next crop appears? Apples, of course.

So if you don't like the outcomes you're getting, your results, then you need to go to the root cause of the problem. This is your mindset.

Think of the roots of the tree as your thoughts.

If you want to see a change it's up to you. You have to change the way you think, in other words, re-programme all the negative associations with being in sales.

Successful selling today and getting to 'yes' is just about helping more people solve their problems and helping them make up their minds.

Ethical selling is about helping people make good decisions, the best decisions for them.

This applies to the teacher or the doctor. It applies to the retail environment or to a business consultant. It applies to selling yourself at an interview and getting someone to give you your first job. Heck, it also applies when you're out on a date, doesn't it?

Selling is simply helping people make up their minds. Most of us need a little help with that and we appreciate it when someone cares enough to help. That's sales.

So reframe what the picture of being in sales looks like to you. Change the words you associate with being in sales.

Try and write a more positive list of associations with being in sales and let's see what you come up with:

Your thoughts create feelings.

These feelings create your actions or in some cases inaction. It is these actions that deliver the results. Get to the root cause of the problem - often your thoughts, if you want to change your results.

R ______________________________

A ______________________________

F ______________________________

T ______________________________

.....

One in the eye for changing your mindset!

The Reluctant Team.

After speaking at an industry conference for opticians and their clinical staff I was approached by the owners of an elite group of the UK's leading independent practices to help with their business growth as a mentor.

The group meet on a regular basis. I facilitate discussions around best practice and provide them with ideas and strategies to boost their sales and profits.

About 9 months into the relationship the owners decided they needed some help putting all the theory I was sharing into practice. They asked me to deliver a sales training day for their combined staff of around 60 people.

Although the idea of increasing sales and profits sits well with the business owners, for clinicians, good Lord, they're not in sales: they're clinicians you know! All the negative words you associated with being in sales are on their lists and they can easily find 20 more too.

I was dealing with the rear guard of the reluctant team here.

When the bosses mentioned the idea of 'up selling' maybe a spare pair of glasses or prescription sun glasses, the clinicians automatically thought nope, we're not in sales, that's only designed to squeeze more money out of the patient in order to put more fuel in the bosses BMW. Nope, we're not in sales. Off went their subconscious minds running the scripts of pushy, slimy etc, etc.

This was going to be a challenge from day one to get them to buy in.

In order to create an effective bespoke training programme I first needed to benchmark their current service and approach to sales. This meant a 'secret shopping' expedition.

I plotted all 10 locations into Google Maps to work out my road trip, then started phoning each one in turn to make an appointment. Oh boy, each call was a revelation to start with.

When did you last call your office and ask for you? OK, I admit that sounds a little nuts. What if you're not yet employed and you're providing potential employers with your mobile number?

Have you checked what happens when someone calls you? How is the phone answered, what crazy message have you got on your voice mail and what impression does it give?

Highlight this or better still write it up on your wall somewhere:

'Inspect what you expect.'

In order that I could benchmark each practice I gave each one of them the same scenario on the phone:

"I'm moving into your area and I've been recommended to your practice. It's been a couple of years since I had an eye test and I'm experiencing slightly blurry vision in my right eye and what I think you know as floaters, little black dots that move around. Can I please book an appointment for an eye test?"

That was it.

Given that these were 10 of the top independent opticians in the country, the quality and professionalism of the way the telephone calls were handled was quite astonishing.

Seriously, inspect what you expect.

With my appointments all made, I packed my bags and the road trip began. I had provided each practice with plenty of information on the telephone in advance of my appointment, agreed?

1. I'm moving into your area.

This provided a great opportunity for an icebreaker, a way to get a conversation going and make the patient feel at ease, an opportunity to build rapport and find out where I was moving from and to.

2. I've been recommended to your practice.

It's great to know who's making recommendations about your services, wouldn't you agree? How nice it would be for the person that made the recommendation just to receive a short handwritten note of thanks. It might even make them think about how they could propagate referrals. How do you put your 'referral team' to work?

3. It's been a couple of years since my last eye test.

As adults we should all have our eyes tested every couple of years. This comment would have allowed the opticians to benchmark my vision from two years ago to the current day.

4. I'm experiencing blurry vision and dark floaters in my right eye.

Whilst I invented the elements of moving into their area and being recommended to them, the blurry vision and floaters in my eye were factual - these needed checking. I also agreed in my own mind that I would say 'yes' to whatever they offered me.

At 10.29 I arrived for my 10.30 appointment at the first of my secret shopping locations.

It was a relatively small practice, very clean tidy and presentable. I approached the rather tall reception desk behind which someone was beavering away on the computer. Eventually they stopped typing, popped their head up over the reception desk/screen and asked,

“Can I help you?”

No shit! Its 10.29. No, it's actually now 10.30 on the dot! Who do you think I am and what do you think I’m here for? It was a small practice, there was only one optometrist who can only see one patient at a time. Who do you think I am?!

Obviously I didn't say that out loud, that would just be too rude, but it was certainly what I was thinking.

“Good morning, my name is Steve Clarke, I'm here for my 10.30 eye test.”

She checked her diary just in case I could have been mistaken.

“Ah yes, Mr Clarke. Which eye test would you like?”

Again, not out loud but in my head I thought, ‘Which eye test? Surely you're the experts, I told you what was wrong when I booked the appointment. Didn’t anybody make a note?’

“I'm not really sure which test do I need?” I asked.

"OK, take a seat please the optometrist will be with you in a moment," and she retreated back behind the safety of her reception desk.

A few moments later the optometrist arrived and ushered me into his room.

"Good morning Mr Clarke, now, you are here for an eye test I understand. How long is it since you had an eye test?"

"A couple of years, I guess"

"OK, we will start with our standardised test. It's £29.95, is that okay?"

"Yes," I said, rather obviously.

Within twenty minutes I was all done. They detected only a minor deterioration in my reading vision and commented that unless it bothered me I'm probably okay with the glasses I have. I thanked them and left.

My experience was much the same for the next three visits. Astonishing really, so far nobody had taken the trouble to record the information I provided over the telephone and relayed that to the people conducting the eye examinations.

Day two and eye test number four.

This time I was greeted with a very smiley, happy young receptionist eager to please.

"Steve Clarke, I'm here for an 11 o'clock appointment."

"Great. Please take a seat Mr Clarke, can I get you a cup of coffee?"

Now this was a new twist, a warm welcome and the offer of a coffee.

"Thank you, that would be lovely."

"Would you like a cappuccino, you know, a frothy one?"

I absolutely loved how this teenager had to explain to the old man, (in her mind), that a new fangled cappuccino was 'the frothy one'.

I sat quietly and enjoyed my cappuccino. I didn't have the heart to tell her it was only lukewarm, but 'A' for effort and enthusiasm.

After a short wait a very junior assistant appeared and invited me in to the examination room.

"Which eye test would you like, Mr Clarke?"

All the good of the cappuccino was instantly undone. What eye test should someone have who's displaying blurry vision and floaters I thought to myself?

"I really don't know. I will need to leave that up to you."

"OK, we'll start with a standardised test which is £29.95, is that alright," he asked.

Oh dear I thought, 'here we go again.'

After the eye test was complete I was then introduced to one of the dispensing opticians who again confirmed there wasn't much change in my vision, but if I did want to change here are the kind of frames they could supply.

I tried so hard to lead him into a sale. I explained what I do for a living. I went on to explain that when I am speaking in front of the room to a group of people I hate looking over the rims of my glasses like an old professor.

He took the bait and introduced me to the idea of varifocal glasses. In simple terms these are glasses with a graduated lens from close-up to distance vision in the same glasses. Ideal for what I described to him.

And yet for some reason he felt duty bound to explain to me all of the downside of the slightly blurry peripheral vision which is inherent with varifocal lenses.

I was still ready to buy, all he had to do was ask and I would say 'yes.' But he just couldn't do it; in his subconscious that would turn him into one of those slippery, sleazy, slimy, pushy, salespeople.

I left. No sale.

By day three I was on eye test number seven and all the way up in Herefordshire.

When did you last have an eye test? I had already had about enough of dark rooms and the repeated questions: better with, better without, better with, better without? But then it all changed. As I walked through the door moments before my allotted appointment I was greeted by friendly receptionists who to my amazement and delight said,

“Good morning, you must be Mr Clarke.”

Hallelujah I thought, someone with enough common sense, or good training, to read their appointment book and anticipate who the person walking through the door might be.

What a warm welcome.

“Take a seat Mr Clarke. You must be quite tired having driven all the way from Essex this morning.”

‘Wow,’ I thought, ‘she's read the notes!’

“I understand you're moving into the area. Where have you been looking?” she asked, with genuine interest.

‘Oh damn!’ Nobody had been asking me up until now I wasn't ready for this.

“Don't ask me, my wife is taking care of all of those details,” I said as a quick recovery.

“You'll love it around here I'm sure. Take a seat. Nina will be with you in a moment.”

And within a few moments Nina appeared. She offered another warm, friendly greeting and ushered me into the examination room.

"Mr Clarke, or may I call you Steve? It says in my notes that you were recommended to us, that's always nice to hear. Who made the recommendation?" she asked.

Nuts! That's two for two. She caught me completely unawares and so I opted to deliver the 'need to check with my wife line' again.

"Steve, I see from your notes that you're reporting blurry vision and floaters in your right eye. How long have you been experiencing that?"

"It must've been three, maybe four months now, nothing major, but I'm aware that looking through my right eye things are blurry and I wouldn't expect them to be and these little floaters are very annoying," I explained.

"I'm sure it's nothing to worry about Steve, but your ocular health is really important to us. I'd like to conduct a thorough eye examination where we can see in, around and behind your eye. Don't worry, this is completely safe and non-invasive. It just lets us get a complete picture and ascertain the health of your eye. It's a little more expensive than a standardised test. It's £89.50. Is that okay?" she asked.

As was my plan, I replied 'yes.'

We positioned ourselves almost eye to eye around the Daytona OCT machine. (Optical Coherence Tomography, just in case you wanted to know).

She focused the machine and commenced with the examination.

She began to fidget rather nervously looking over the machine at me and then back through the equipment once more.

Again she looked over the machine at me, this time I could see a small bead of sweat appear on her forehead then she looked back to the machine once more.

She sat back and rather nervously said, "Mr Clarke, just a moment, I'll be right back," and left in a hurry.

'Mr Clarke,' I thought to myself? 'A moment ago I was Steve, what's up?'

Within two minutes Nina came back into the room.

"Mr Clarke. Please don't panic."

When somebody says don't panic what do you immediately do? Panic!

"Mr Clarke, we have called the A&E department and we have a car waiting for you downstairs. We're taking you to the hospital right now as *your retina is detaching*."

'What?!?!'

My initial thought was does she not know I'm secret shopping? And then I thought… she sounds serious so best to go along with this. Within minutes I was walking through the doors of the A&E department at the general hospital. There was no long wait that I would normally associate with a visit to an A&E department.

"Mr Clarke, come straight through."

I sat with a similar machine to the one the optometrist had used between me and the consultant on call. As he set the machine into action, he said, "Looks like a retinal detachment alright; when did you last eat Mr Clarke?"

Now this sounds serious I thought. This sounds like the precursor to an operation. Perhaps it's best that I explain what I've been doing the last few days.

"Could what you're looking at through the machine possibly be the result of the fact that I've had seven eye tests in the last three days?" I asked.

He looked at me with an extremely puzzled look on his face as if to say, you've done what?

OK, It's best that I come clean I thought.

"I've been running a secret shopping program for some of the top opticians in the country. As a result of this, over the last three days I've now had seven eye tests, could this have caused any problems that you're maybe seeing now?" I asked out of all innocence.

With an even more puzzled look on his face the consultant asked, "Are you secret shopping now?"

"Hold on, is my retina detaching?" I almost shouted back at him.

"Yes," he replied.

"Then I'm not secret shopping anymore!"

When your retina begins to detach it falls away from your eye gathering speed like wet wallpaper coming away from the wall. If it fully detaches you're blind. If it's detected in time your sight can be saved.

A long and painful story short, after three lengthy operations the sight in my right eye was saved.

Almost 4 months after the secret shopping exercise began it was time to meet 60 staff from the independent practices for what they believed to be sales training day. As very 'reluctant sales teams', sales training was the last thing they wanted or felt they needed.

To kick the morning session off I delivered the blow by blow results of the secret shopping expedition.

I kept it light-hearted as there was nothing to be gained from a name and shame session. The delegates clapped and cheered one another as my story moved from branch to branch.

"And then I got to Hereford." I paused for dramatic effect.

Everybody started laughing assuming I was about to rip into the staff from Hereford. The laughing immediately turned to a stunned silence the moment I mentioned the words 'detached retina'.

I let them sit with their thoughts for what must have felt like an eternity; in reality it was just a couple of seconds, to let the severity sink in. The silence was eventually broken by one of the business owners.

"That's disgusting. We run some of the top practices in the country; we should all have equipment to be able to detect a detached retina," he exclaimed.

"No, that's not the problem; you all have the equipment. What's disgusting is that some of you were prepared to let me go blind instead of selling me the appropriate test. What's disgusting is you would have let me go blind for the sake of £60. Had you all listened and acted upon the indicators I provided and not worried about "up selling" me from £29 to £89 for the eye test, you all could have detected my detached retina."

I left them in silence for a few moments more. We ran the exercise of capturing the words people use to describe someone being in sales that you did earlier in this book. We then set about reframing what sales means to them.

Unanimously they agreed that if their mother, husband or brother were displaying the symptoms that I had displayed they would have no hesitation in saying, sit down, shut up, take a credit card out, it's a more expensive test, but you're having it because...

They all agreed that they are there to serve. And if they're not providing the right service and best advice possible they are not serving fully.

We had a major breakthrough during the morning session when someone pointed out, with honesty, that they have an issue with what they knew at their branch as 'up selling'.

The breakthrough came when one of the team said we need to change the way we think of this - it is not 'up selling'; it is **'up serving'** - brilliant!

Up-serve your clients from this day forwards.

Up-serve your co-workers, your family, your friends. Help them more, help them the best way you possibly can and you'll see a win-win all round.

Reframe what being in sales looks like. If you're a member of the reluctant sales team know that helping people and serving them better is all that being in sales is really all about.

Remind yourself. We're all in sales to some degree.

We're either in the Regular, the Reluctant or the Referral team, but we're all in sales.

Whatever happens today, tomorrow or the next day, to get to 'yes' more often and achieve your goals, set your subconscious and conscious mind to work and repeat this affirmation over and over.

Find a way, don't find an excuse.

Eureka moments in finding a way

* Success leaves clues

* Knowledge isn't power

* Don't worry about asking for advice

* It's important to become a great leader

* Get out of your comfort zone

* Don't live in the past

* Surround yourself with positive people

* WTF … Where's The Focus?

* We're all in sales - get over it

* The Regular, The Reluctant…and The Referral teams

* Your thoughts create feelings, actions and results

* Inspect what you expect

* Upserve your clients from this day forwards

In the next chapter we are going to look into the First "E" in the *EUREKA* acronym, it's all about Engagement. Are you ready? OK, let's crack on.

Chapter 2

EUREKA

Engage a hungry audience

'When people are financially invested, they want a return. When people are emotionally invested, they want to contribute.'
Simon Sinek

To get to 'yes' today you must learn to engage your audience; preferably one with a hunger for whatever you have on offer.

Are you familiar with the term ROI (Return on Investment)? It's been a staple of the business world for years. In simple terms it's a measure used to determine the investment gain on the capital invested.

Now I've explained it, forget it. I'd like you to scrap that idea for now and replace ROI with ROE. In my world this stands for Return on Engagement.

To succeed in business today you must find every opportunity to Engage with your clients, prospects and co-workers.

To have a happy marriage or great relationship you should also consider your ROE. When you're with your wife/husband/significant other, be present, be there. Engage in eye contact, engage in conversation. Ask great questions and listen, in other words - engage.

Don't sit over a romantic dinner looking at your phone, texting or checking Facebook (and we've all seen couples doing it) - engage. Or you might find they are texting someone else! Engage, because you care, and you will reap the rewards.

**Switch your thinking from ROI to ROE –
Return on Engagement.**

People today value and take more notice of a conversation not a publication. Broadcasting your message the old world way just doesn't cut it.

The world has changed. In the digital age we're all more connected than at any other time in history, and yet paradoxically we are disconnected.

To get someone's attention it is far more important that we stop trying to broadcast our messages. We're bombarded by advertising messages every minute of every day, so much so that we consciously, and even subconsciously, screen them out.

.....

A pivotal moment in time.

On January 20th 2009, Barack Hussein Obama II defeated Republican nominee John McCain and was sworn in as the 44th President of the United States of America.

During the usual extensive election campaigning, Obama had been promising 'change' during many of his stirring speeches. Whatever your political persuasion, few can deny the great oratory skills of President Obama.

Well, we got a change, in fact, a very obvious and visible one. For the first time in history America had a mixed race president.

But, as far as we're all concerned, that was not the most relevant change to affect us all.

The most relevant change I want to draw your attention to did not occur with Obama taking office. Nor did the change occur with Bush coming into or leaving office. However, Bush leaving office did create a fantastic opportunity for one of my all-time favourite adverts to run in various newspapers.

I love this. Perhaps the final humiliation for George Bush; being used to advertise a ladies' hair removal product.

04 | news

History in the making

Aussies on the spot

Actions speak

Les Carlyon

Goodbye Bush

Veet

www.veet.com.au

The now famous Veet 'Goodbye Bush' quarter page ad ran in Sydney's *Daily Telegraph* and Melbourne's *Herald Sun* with coverage of President Barack Obama's inauguration and the farewell of George W. Bush.

The ad gained worldwide acclaim after it was spread virally over the internet (which is where my ramblings are taking us in a moment).

The ad soon took on a life of its own; being scanned and sent around the world by both the general public and the ad industry.

The brand awareness did no harm for Veet at all; people enjoyed the light hearted, suggestive humour. Sales of the product went through the roof! The return on their investment came not from the advert itself, but from their Return On Engagement.

Electing the first mixed race president was monumental, but it's not the biggest change I'm talking about.

I believe that one of the biggest changes to affect us all today actually occurred during President Clinton's time in office.

Clinton was inaugurated as the 42nd President of the United States on January 20, 1993.

Just a few years before he took office, during the Christmas period of 1990, little known British computer scientist, Tim Berners-Lee, had assembled all the tools necessary for a working version of the first World Wide Web. The biggest change since the industrial revolution had occurred and **the world had changed forever.**

Think back if you can, and you're old enough, to January 1993. Many of us will remember the time Bill Clinton became President after all, it's really not that long ago. On the day he took office there was somewhere in the order of just 600 websites in existence. When he left the White House in 2001, just 8 years later there were over 36,000,000 websites!! Read that again, that's over 36 million sites!

The world had changed and we're not going back.

"When I took office, only high energy physicists had ever heard of what is called the World Wide Web. Now even my cat has its own page."

This was Bill Clinton's announcement of the Next Generation Internet initiative, 1996.

.....

A quantum shift from scarcity to abundance.

Again, cast your minds back, if you can, and if you're too young to remember, ask your mum or dad.

When we watched TV we had the equivalent of today's *X Factor (Opportunity Knocks)* or the equivalent of *I'm a Celebrity (3-2-1* and Dusty Bin). Seriously, if you haven't heard of *3-2-1* check it out on YouTube - you won't believe the rubbish we used to watch.

On a Saturday evening, I'd sit and watch the host of *3-2-1* Ted Rodgers and the star of the show, Dusty Bin, and try and figure out what on earth was going on. I'd think... it's going to get better, it's going to get better. It never got better.

There was little alternative to Saturday night TV entertainment at that time.

How many channels did we have back then, can you remember? There were only four channels to choose from. How many are there now? Hundreds! We've moved from scarcity to abundance. Back then, we had to watch it whilst it was live. The majority of TV sets didn't even have a remote control. Imagine! The scarcity of channels made us easy targets for advertisers.

With viewing numbers for these shows hitting a whopping 18 million on a Saturday night it was an advertising company's dream come true. Companies could buy their time and shout their messages to the masses. Any of today's TV shows would die for viewer figures like these. Nowadays we can record any one of hundreds of channels from around the world. We can pause live TV. We can watch programs on our laptops when we want to and catch up on anything we missed over the internet.

What do we do when the adverts come on? Fast forward! Every time.

You can't just keep SHOUTING your sales messages the old fashioned way and hope to be heard above the noise, and I mean shouting in any form of advertising. You need to be finding new ways of engaging with your clients and prospects. The move from a scarcity of channels to an abundance of channels and viewing methods means marketing yourself, your products or services needs to change.

.....

Remember, to keep doing what you've always done and just hope for better results is the definition of insanity.

Back in the '90's who did you go to for your electricity? The Electricity Board! What was the choice? Now you can choose from any number of suppliers. You can even get your electricity from British Gas!

Who was your telephone line supplier? In the UK - BT. What was the choice? None. Now we have all manner of suppliers. In fact, many people don't even have landlines now as there are so many mobile options.

In each case it's the choice that makes the difference. The abundance of choice. So with the advent of the W.W.W we moved to a position of abundance in terms of information.

Back in the '90's if you needed a tenancy agreement drawn up there was only one place you could go - a solicitor. Today, if you need a simple legal contract where do you go? The internet. And you very likely enter your requirements into the search bar in Google.

Anything you want to know, anything you want to find, anything you want to see; it's all there online, one click away and available in seconds. Now with smart phones, laptops and tablets this information is at our finger tips any time, any place, anywhere.

The world has changed. Have you?

'The price of doing the same old thing is far higher than the price of change.'

Bill Clinton

.....

Why a new approach is so important.

Firstly, are we on the same page? Do you take my point of how people are screening out advertising these days? OK.

Not all advertising of course, some still gets through, like the Veet advert, for example, but we are set to screen out so much of the 'noise' these days. People don't like being advertised at, so you need to find new ways to engage with more people in your target market and hold their attention. You need to stand out from the crowd.

Let people get to know you, like you and trust you – that way, when they're ready to buy they come to you and ask for what you have on offer.

The question is, how do you do this? Are you standing out from the crowd for the right reasons? Are you visible and attractive? Admittedly it's easier for some than others.

As I travel the world speaking at various business events, some people I encounter definitely stand out from the crowd more than others. Some for the right reasons and sadly some for the wrong ones.

The challenge is the same for practically every entrepreneur and business owner I meet right now. What can you do to find more of the right kind of clients, make more sales and more profit?

Yet I'm staggered by the number of people that still insist on doing things the same old way and hope for better results. There are others that feel driven to follow the herd and hope for sales to roll in. Or prospective job hunters who send out a standard bland CV and hope to get the interview.

Wake up folks. That's never going to happen.

Why keep repeating a pattern that's not working for you? That's mad!

.....

For things to change you need to change.

I've said it before, and I'll keep saying it until the message hits home, in case you haven't noticed the world has changed and we're not going back. How many companies do you know that are 'up-sizing'? Or like me, do you see more 'down-sizing' going on?

Now, thanks to technology it's possible to become more efficient and automate many elements of business to reduce costs and improve efficiencies. If you move with the times.

Here's one rule I've always tried to apply when looking for ways to succeed in business, in sales and in life:

'Follow the leaders, don't follow the followers'.

Find who's getting the results you want and latch on to them. Don't just follow the herd.

I had to laugh out loud each time I went to the men's toilets at a business show in Earls Court, London… no, stop it, I'm serious!

First visit of the day and the facilities were nice and clean and tidy. Mid-morning and someone had decided that this was a great place to advertise their web design services. They'd spread their cards around the sinks and on shelves above the urinals.

Within no time at all the desperate herd mentality kicked in. Everyone else who was struggling for leads saw this as a free opportunity to 'advertise'. Really? In the men's toilets. Do me a favour.

What does this say about your products and services? If you're selling cleaning products or sanitary wear, maybe. But legal services, book keeping, web design and printing – all scattering their cards and flyers (which they paid good money for) around the men's room almost begging for business.

To rise above the crowd and win more business you need to become "visible and attractive." There are so many ways to do this, but for most of us littering the public toilets definitely isn't the way to do it.

Trying to attract the attention of your target audience by buying the same old advertising in newspapers and magazines and just hoping people see it is not going to cut it, not anymore.

We need to work on **Engagement** and at every opportunity you have to consider how you can engage people in conversation rather than sending your message via a publication or flyers in the toilets!

Take a minute or two now to jot down at least 10 or 12 touch points where you have the opportunity to engage with your clients, your potential employer or your dream partner.

And then also, I'd like you to consider the hat you'd be wearing at that time: is it your regular, your reluctant or your referral team hat?

What are the touch points that you've got? Did you think about social media? What are you doing to engage people rather than broadcast? Are you broadcasting on Twitter and Facebook, or engaging people in conversation?

'I just had a cheese sandwich' . Ping!

Nobody cares.

Are you asking questions? Are you sharing valuable or helpful information?

Remember, it's ROE not ROI.

.....

The Law of Reciprocity

Okay, let me explain to you what I mean by the law of reciprocity if you're unfamiliar with the term. There's an unwritten rule that if you help other people, human nature being what it is, they naturally want to reciprocate and do something for you in return if they can.

How can you help others instead of thinking of your needs and wants first?

We are in the grips of global trust crisis. A question you should be asking yourself on a regular basis is how can you add value to other people, other businesses, clients and how can you build trust? How can you show you care about them?

Remember this:

People don't care how much you know, until they know how much you care.

I would urge you now to think about people that you could help by way of an introduction, someone you could help with a recommendation to another product or service you've used that would help them.

However, I'd like you to think about this without expecting things in return because the law of reciprocity just happens. Trust me on this; it just happens.

I'm an avid user of LinkedIn. Please feel free to send me a connection request - you never know who I might have in my network that I could connect you with.

You'll find my profile here:

https://uk.linkedin.com/in/motivationalbusinessspeaker/

Each day I review LinkedIn to see who has looked at my profile. In return I have a quick look at their profile and decide if there's anything that immediately springs to mind that I could help them with. If I know someone I think I should introduce them to or if I know of a product, a website or an app the might be of interest to them then I send them a message to that effect.

If I see there is something obvious I could help them with, get ready for this. Are you ready, because this is pure gold.

I pick up the phone and call them. It's not a cold call, I'm calling to help them, I'm not calling to sell them anything!

With this mindset, even the reluctant team can think like an optician and up serve, agreed? If I have information that would be helpful to them, I feel that I owe it to the other party to share this information.

Here's an example of precisely what happened with one experience I had on LinkedIn.

I noticed that a young lady named Marija had viewed my profile. Marija is from Macedonia and she runs an events organisation business. I was intrigued by her profile and followed the link through to her website. It clearly showed that her company puts on great business events all across Europe on a range of topics. It also showed that she books international business speakers... I'm an international business speaker.

Before you read on, consider what you would do in this situation, and be honest.

Would you do nothing, because you never review those who look at your profile? You really shouldn't admit to this one, whether you're in business for yourself, looking for your first job, or looking for a career progression because LinkedIn is a goldmine.

If you're not a first level connection would you send them a connection request?

Would you send them a message via Inmail (LinkedIn's internal email system).

Would you find her personal email address and approach them that way?

What would you do?

Here's what I did. I found a telephone number for Maria on her business website. I saw that she is based in Macedonia, checked the internet to see the time difference and then picked up the phone and called her.

I don't speak Macedonian! As an Englishman I feel blessed; the predominant business language around the world is English. What's the worst thing that could happen on such a phone call? I might not be understood. That might be awkward for a moment, but it won't be the end of the world for the person I'm calling or indeed for me.

I didn't call and launch into a sales pitch. I didn't call to say that 'I see that you book speakers, I'm a speaker book me.' That would be a dreadful sales pitch and it would be all about me. I called to see if I could help her in any way.

Here's how the phone call went:

"Good morning, please may I speak to Marija?"

"May I ask who is calling?"

Brilliant, I thought, whoever is on the phone in Macedonia

speaks perfect English.

“Yes, my name is Steve Clarke and I'm calling from England. Is Marija available please?”

“Oh, thank you for calling Steve, this is Marija speaking.” She couldn't hide her surprise.

“Marija, I was wondering if you have just a couple of moments to talk right now?”

“Yes, of course.”

“Please don't freak out Marija, but I can see that you were looking at my profile on LinkedIn. I see from your profile and from your website that you're very active in the business events industry. I know lots of really great business speakers and would be delighted to make any recommendations to you if there’s anything in particular you are looking for.”

“Thank you Steve, that's very kind of you, but I was looking at your profile because I would like to discuss the possibility of you speaking for me in Macedonia.”

Bingo!

But don't expect the law of reciprocity to kick in quite that quickly every single time!

Since that first booking in Macedonia I have worked with Marija in Serbia, Kosovo, Romania, Bulgaria, Poland, Latvia,

Lithuania, Prague and I am already back on round two in Macedonia with the rest to follow.

I have also introduced Marija to a number of other great speakers who have also been working all across Eastern Europe with her too.

We have become trusted business partners and great friends. I was so deeply honoured to even be invited to her wedding! I think it's safe to say this is when you know you've built a business relationship on 'know, like and trust'.

Here's another real life example for you on a local and personal level.

.....

Numb toes and the law of reciprocity

I'm no marathon runner, in fact I've never really been a runner at all. As a kid I had such severe asthma that even a relatively small amount of exercise would result in me requiring immediate rest and oxygen at home or even hospitalisation.

My wife, Susanne, however, is quite an athlete; she's run the London Marathon four times now and thinks nothing of a casual 10km run.

Three years ago, I decided that I too should be able to run a 10km race. 10km, that's only 6.2 miles, how tough could that be? I was about to find out.

Knowing the cross country route was the local 10km run, I took off. I went for a solo trial run like 'Macho Man' with, no warmup, training, or preparation. The disastrous result was inevitable.

The next day I found myself in hospital not through asthma, I'm all done with that, thank goodness, but I found myself needing an emergency operation on a torn cartilage in my knee!

As I'm writing this, my knee is now okay again, and I'm determined that this September I will complete my first official 10km run.

I've been documenting my progress towards it quite openly on Facebook. The support and encouragement has been fantastic.

This time it's been a slow, steady buildup to avoid injury; 2km, 3km, 5km, back to 2km and repeat... run, walk, run, walk.

In one post recently I mentioned the fact that I was getting numb toes during my run and in came lots of advice, all well-meaning and appreciated, but I want to share two things that happened that you could benefit from in business too.

They were two things that ultimately invoked 'the law of reciprocity'.

Remember, you do something for somebody they reciprocate, but you do it without expectation.

The first was a post from Danny Gosshawk, the owner at Pure Body Health. Dan is a physiotherapist, he's someone who's looked after me in the past through all manner of aches and pains.

"Drop in for a free MOT Steve, let's see if we can work out what the problem is with the toes," offered Dan.

Another message was from Stuart Carmichael, he's the owner of Flitch Bikes, a speciality bike shop in Great Dunmow. Stu's not only a mad keen cyclist, but has been an active and very competitive triathlete too.

"Drop-by the shop Steve; let me check how you're lacing your running shoes," came the suggestion from Stu.

Think about that, he owns a cycle shop, not a running shop, yet is offering to help me lace my running shoes, (no, not because I can't tie a lace as I'm used to Velcro, but there are special techniques apparently for running shoes. I never knew!)

They were both genuinely looking after my interests, not expecting anything in return. When was the last time you did this for clients or contacts you have?

Try this for yourself this week. Look for someone who you could help with some advice or introduction at no charge; but think of something that would help them, not just serve you.

I visited both Dan and Stu. They both freely gave me their time, help and advice without expectation or charge.

Dan gave me a full hour's MOT, as he called it: a physical health check from head to toe.

He created an entire stretching routine to help loosen my muscles in the hope of reducing the numb toes. As a really nice touch (no pun intended as he's a great massage therapist too) he sent me a video message follow up with photographs of each stretch and a message of encouragement too. Brilliant.

That's when the law of reciprocity kicked in for him.

I called and booked a number of sports massages with Dan at full price. Did he advertise at me? No. Did he sell to me? No. Did I buy? Yes!

I then dropped in on Stu. He stopped what he was doing and checked out my running shoes before spending time lacing them in a way that would give me more room in the width of my shoes. Again with no charge or expectation.

Two days later I dropped off my road bike at his shop for him to service whilst I was away on holiday. Did he advertise at me? No. Did he sell to me? No. Did I buy? Yes!

Now see if you can invoke the law of reciprocity this week as well.

I'd urge you to make it part of your routine every day to look at who you could help because the more you help, the more good stuff will come your way.

One of the questions I get asked a lot from a sales perspective is how can I engage with prospects without being a nuisance?

Well, if the only thing you do is call up your prospects and say, ‘Are you ready to buy? Are you ready to buy yet? I’ ll give you 20% off if you buy now!’ If you do this you have no chance.

Stop all that and think about how could you help those people without expecting something back in return. Think if you were them, what problem have you got? How could someone you know outside of your own company, or the products or services you provide, be really helpful to them?

Write down a list of at least six or eight people that you think you could help. Just brainstorm it on your own or with someone on your team. Think about who could you help and how could you help them? Who could you introduce to another person or company? What could genuinely help them?

Eureka moments in the first E of EUREKA

*** Engage a hungry audience**

*** Switch your thinking from ROI to ROE**

*** *Goodbye Bush* - a pivotal moment in time**

*** The world has changed and we're not going back**

*** A quantum shift from scarcity to abundance**

*** Broadcasting your message doesn't work anymore**

*** Move from publication to conversation**

*** The law of reciprocity**

*** Use Linkedin, but also pick up the phone**

So the first 'E' in EUREKA stands for Engagement.

Broadcasting your message the old way simply won't cut it today.

Engage with your target audience, serve your target audience, help your target audience.

The next chapter is the 'U' in EUREKA. In order to get to 'yes' more often you need to Uncover the pain or problem in their life or in their world. Your mission then is to help them find a solution. Let's crack on!

Chapter 3

EUREKA

Uncover the pain

'The secret to success is learning how to use pain and pleasure, instead of having pain and pleasure use you'.
Tony Robbins

It's human nature that the vast majority of people in the world are driven away from pain towards pleasure.

Yes, yes, I know there's a group of people who are driven towards the pleasure they get from pain, but that's a completely different subject and not one that we're going to cover today!

This fundamental pain versus pleasure principle lies at the heart of pretty much everything we do. Your beliefs, values and the life rules you set for yourself are all built around this basic principle. The decisions you make, the actions you take and the habits that you form are pretty much all based on pain versus pleasure.

We've all heard the expression 'no pain no gain'. Well that may be true for your workout in the gym as in short-term pain for longer term gain.

Before you make any decision you unconsciously ask yourself the following questions:

What does this mean?

Will the result of this lead to pain or pleasure?

What action should I take?

Each decision you then make will lead to one or more of these particular consequences:

1. short-term pain
2. short-term pleasure
3. long-term pain
4. long-term pleasure

There will also be a varying degree of intensity of the pain or the pleasure ranging from low to high. The higher the intensity the more influence it has on your decision. On the flip side is that the lower the intensity the less impact it is like to have on your decision-making process.

It’s probably why so many diets fail. Actually I should rephrase that. It's not usually the diet that fails at all. It's more likely that you have not put enough emphasis on the pain of eating an unhealthy diet or lack of exercise and being hugely overweight. I know this from my first-hand experience.

I had allowed myself to slip into a somewhat sedentary lifestyle. At the age of 56 I found myself tipping the scales at 92 kg (14.5 stone). That would not be considered morbidly obese, but for my frame and my height of 5’7” it was at least 12 kg (2 stone) over my healthy weight and I was feeling the ill effects.

I felt tired all the time. My joints ached, my back ached and after climbing a few flights of stairs I'd be short of breath. I hated the feeling.

‘None of us are getting any younger,’ people would say.

That might be true, but on the whole we’re all living longer. Our life expectancy is now far greater than our grandparents and even our parents.

Heck, my dad is now 89 and still plays golf twice a week and walks the course! From that gene pool and the advances in medical science I’m very likely to see a hundred years myself.

Susanne and I have five children between us, and now two grandchildren, with with many more to come, no doubt. I had to get myself in shape for my own well-being and for my family.

I made some firm decisions based around short-term pain and long-term pleasure.

I cut out the chocolate, cheese and wine from my diet. No, that would be a lie. I massively cut down on the intake of these three. I stepped up the intake of healthy food including fresh fruit and I cut out all processed food, and foods high in sugar and salt. Plus, I consciously reduced my portion sizes at mealtimes.

Understanding this pain-pleasure principle means that you have more chance of successfully being able to adjust your levels of motivation as you work towards your goals. When it comes to finding peak levels of motivation it all comes down to how much pain-pleasure you associate to achieving or not achieving your goal.

Another decision that I made definitely involved some short-term pain: regular daily exercise. This was full of short-term pain I can tell you. I mentioned earlier in the book that I suffered from a torn cartilage after attempting my first 10km run. This time with my eye firmly on the prize of being lighter and healthier I began a workout plan that involved a slow buildup. Stretch, run, walk, run, walk, run, walk, stretch.

Steadily over time my distance increased as did my stamina. The pain subsided and became pleasure. I never thought I would say this, but I now love to go running.

I feel fitter and healthier than I have for many, many years. As I sit here, I still have a little way to go with my weight loss, but I have managed to shed 10 kg (1.57 stone) and it is still falling.

In order to achieve this milestone I had to consider what would prevent me from moving forwards. In doing so I had to associate more pain with being overweight and unfit in my mind than the pleasure I derived from the lifestyle choices I had been making.

The decisions you make will then depend on how you personally interpret pain versus pleasure in your life or the business situation that this decision relates to.

Essentially, people are driven away from pain towards pleasure. To help you get a 'yes' with a personal goal or a 'yes' from a client or prospect in business, you need to understand the pain involved in doing or not doing something.

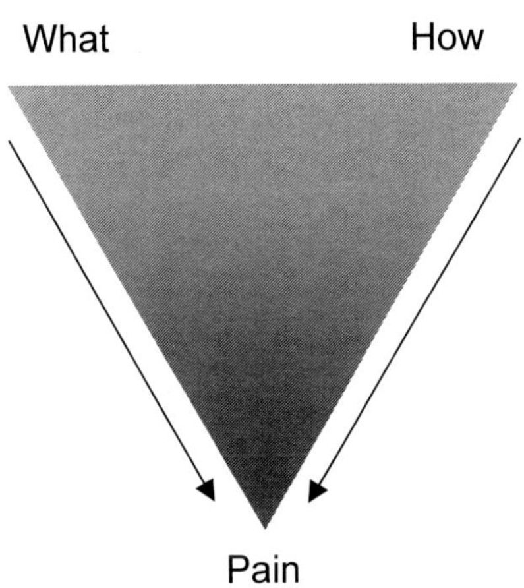

In a business situation we need to connect at either a financial, personal or emotional level in order for them to recognise and feel the pain. Let me show you what I mean.

Allow me to introduce you to the *Eureka Impact Triangle* as I call it.

Let's assume you're in IT sales and you meet someone at a business networking event and they tell you they've got to change all of their IT systems. You think bingo! A buying signal, they want to change, right?

Well, of course, but there's not enough pain attached to why they've got to change and if you don't get to the pain all they're going to ask you is 'how much?' And you probably don't want to be a 'how much?' kind of a company because all you do then is compete on price.

If you want to maintain margins, you need to get to the pain and the impact of that pain on the person you're talking to and to their business. At the tip of the triangle is the pain point. You need to dig in by questioning people about what that means and how it affects them.

There's a 'what' and there's a 'how' question at the top of the triangle. We need to use the what and how questions to dig deeper to understand where the real pain is.

'So, you've got to change your IT system; what's the impact, right now, financially, on the business of keeping the systems you've got?'

'What kind of stress and strain does this cause around the office?'

'If the systems continue breaking down what kind of impact does this have on you as the IT manager?'

We're looking for the real pain and a connection at an emotional level.

I know that some people are already feeling a little uncomfortable because this sounds maybe a little 'salesy' but you owe it to yourself and to the clients to get to where the real pain is because it is only then that you can be the source of salvation. You are the person that can help them solve that problem.

Do you remember the optometrist story? Asking good questions, finding the real source of the pain and the problem is the best possible way that you can upserve your clients.

We buy with emotion and justify with logic.

You will find the 'impact triangle' a useful tool in getting to 'yes' more often.

.....

Hitting the right pain points for your niche.

Do you understand what I mean by a niche market?

Because if you're not niched with your product or your service, again, all that people can say to you is 'how much?' Because if you haven't found the pain that we talked about previously, you haven't established a firm connection with them at an emotional level. You haven't motivated them to buy from you yet because you very likely haven't built strong rapport, you haven't shown you understand their problem and you haven't shown that you care.

What is your principal niche?

Principal niche? Well, that sounds like good news as it implies you can have more than one niche - good news - you can have several niches. But why is this so important? You've heard this before I'm sure, but why is it so important to focus on niche markets?

I was an owner and director of an IT parts company. Not a very sexy business, but quite a profitable one. We were suppliers of spare parts to the computer trade predominantly for laptops.

To keep a long story short, we spotted an opportunity to create a very niche proposition for the insurance claims market in the UK.

Through a chance conversation with a client who had a damaged laptop we discovered that IT related claims created a real problem and major pain financially and from the stress of the workload for insurance claims teams up and down the country. Stressed out claims teams were delivering substandard service in a highly competitive market. That was a real pain with a potentially huge negative impact.

We became an outsourced call handling and supply centre for IT related insurance claims.

If you dropped your laptop you would call your insurance company and they would appoint us to handle the claim. We would collect and inspect the equipment and then repair or replace as necessary. We were able to deliver a much higher level of service because of our understanding of the technology. We improved efficiencies, often reduced costs, then having uncovered the pain of both the insurance company and the insured party we built trust and solved problems.

As a result of focusing on a niche we built a strong reputation in the marketplace. We were no longer just an IT parts company selling odd spare parts around the country. We experienced something very exciting in business, it's known as *step growth*.

As we rolled out our proposition to the marketplace, we won contract after contract until we had all of the top 10 insurers in the UK on our books. We had found a solution to the pain in a niche market.

In just eight years we grew the company to annual revenues in excess of £32 million. We owned our niche. We were listed as a Times top 100 fastest-growing SME companies in the UK before achieving a successful multi-million pound exit.

This is what can happen when you remove the pain within a niche market!

To get to ‘yes’ you must give careful consideration as to what kind of niche you want to appeal to. This again applies to your personal life, your career or the business you’re in.

If you're in business, have a look at your website. Is the message clear as to whom you want to appeal to? Do people know they’re on the right website the moment they arrive? Does the copy and the imagery let them identify with their niche or are you trying a one-size-fits-all?

Are you a generalist or a specialist? Who can command the higher price in business, a generalist or a specialist? Obviously the specialist.

If you're circulating your CV for your ideal position, does it reflect to the niche that you want to appeal to? Have you made reference to the fact that you understand the problems and challenges in that particular industry? Would employing you move your target employer away from pain and towards pleasure?

What niche or niches should you be focusing on? What pain can you relieve? Capture your thoughts now.

So when you've got your niches down, maybe you've identified multiple niches. This will help you create the avatar of your 'ideal clients'.

An awful lot of people have got time wasters in their business. The tyre kickers that never actually buy.

Have you got time wasters in your business? I hate to be so blunt, but it's probably your fault. Many businesses set their marketing up to attract all and sundry, they are focused on generating as many enquiries as they can; quantity over quality and, in my opinion, that's wrong.

Think of marketing like a magnet. A magnet does two things, it attracts and it repels.

If you're marketing is attracting the wrong kind of prospects, the chances are you've got your marketing magnet on suck, when in fact you may need to learn to blow more. You're attracting everyone and anyone when it would be far better to repel some of the time wasters. The way to do that is to clearly identify your niche and within your niches to clearly identify the profiles of your ideal clients.

If you're already in business run a review. Who are your best clients currently? Where can you make a good profit and who are the least hassle to deal with? In fact, how about who are the ones that are a pleasure to deal with?

Once you've modelled your ideal client profile then you can afford to jettison the nuisance ones, the troublesome ones, so that you can focus on attracting more profitable, pleasurable clients to 'up serve'.

Consider what happens when you prune a rosebush in the garden. When you prune back hard the good stuff can flourish.

What's the profile of your ideal client in each of your niches? Look at their demographics: age, sex, geographical location, etc.

You should also create a profile based on their psychographic. Get inside the minds of these people and think what else they like to buy, what aspirations do they have? What kind of car they drive and why? How do they dress? What music do they listen to? Try to understand more about their mindset and what excites them.

This means that when you are creating imagery and copy for your website or you're at a meeting talking to these 'ideal prospects', you're putting yourself in the right place, in the right way, and you'll find more of the right kind of clients are automatically attracted to you.

This works in your personal and social life too, doesn't it? Birds of a feather flock together.

.....

Could you relieve pain through innovation?

Wednesday 9th March 2016, 5.30am. It's cold, dark and raining outside. I'm leaving a friend's house in central London and heading for Paddington Station for a train to Cardiff to see one of my clients.

I could walk the streets and get soaked in the rain and hope to hail a black cab, the traditional black cab, the solution we've had in London for years and years without a change. What a pain. Is there an alternative? Of course there is.

Times change and things move on. In all areas of our lives we see innovation.

I open the Uber app on my phone. It instantly knows where I am.

I tap the screen and in real time I can see where the nearest cab is. I can see who my potential driver is, the registration of the car and the type of vehicle.

One more tap and he's on his way and I can watch on the screen on my phone and see as he rounds the corner and pulls up at the front door.

They may not have 'the knowledge' after ages spent on the streets on their moped studying maps and routes (no wonder most black cabbies bitch and moan by nature) but Uber taxis do all have sat nav's. Times have changed.

When we pull up at Paddington no cash changes hands; it's all taken care of via the app and the receipt hits my email inbox. Done.

It all works for the consumer, for the customer and it makes things simple and efficient, it takes away the pain and delivers pleasure.

Meanwhile at Paddington, the black cabs all wait in line getting ready for their next customer to be handed to them.

It will be a while, but at least they will have more to complain about by the time they get their next passenger.

How are you innovating in your industry and in your everyday life? Are you just doing the same old things, the same old ways, just hoping for better results?

Are you leaving it to chance or making it happen? Are you innovating? Businesses that treat change like the enemy will hit the wall and will fail. It's just a matter of time.

On the train journey to Cardiff I had time to reflect on the Uber experience. It made me realise there was a new and exciting way to innovate with the client I was heading to see. We could take the Uber style solution into their industry and totally shake things up. We are set to disrupt that market, in a good way. Right now I can't say anymore, all very top secret!

I dare you to think differently. I dare you to find the pain and shake things up. Innovation doesn't have to be technology led, it can be service driven. It could be a current system rethought, re-engineered. When you create and live with a 'yes' culture you're always on the look out for creating positive change. Go forth, find the pain and disrupt!

Eureka moments in the U of EUREKA

* People move away from pain and towards pleasure

* Use the Eureka Pain Triangle

* People buy with emotion and justify with logic

* Hit the right pain points for your niche

* Can you relieve the pain through innovation?

* Shake things up and disrupt

That's the U in EUREKA - uncover the pain. If you don't find the pain it's difficult to get people motivated to move.

Remember to dig deep with questioning. If you don't find the true pain you won't make an impact.

In the next chapter we look at more key ingredients of how to create a 'yes' culture in your business and in your life. We will be looking at the vital element of building Rapport and how to extend and multiply your Reach.

Ready? Let's go.

Chapter 4

EUREKA

Rapport and Reach

'The single biggest problem in communication is the illusion that it has taken place.'
George Bernard Shaw

Rapport

Have you have noticed that some people seem to have a knack for connecting with other people? Whoever they meet, they manage to create a sense of trust and understanding within a matter of minutes.

You may believe this is a natural gift that they possess. However, I don't think this is the case. I believe that developing rapport is a skill that anyone can learn, develop, and use effectively and I don't mean in any underhand or manipulative way.

If you're trying to build rapport just to sell something to someone that they wouldn't otherwise want or need or that will do them harm, this is obviously wrong, cynical, and manipulative. Look back at the checklist of the negative words associated in many people's minds with salespeople and you'll see precisely what I mean.

Being in rapport is to have a genuine, close harmonious relationship in which the people or groups concerned understand each other's feelings and emotions and communicate well.

In simple terms, there is a mutual liking and trust when you are in rapport with someone or in rapport with a group. Once you've established rapport that person is more likely to be open and share information with you. When in rapport, the trust and openness flows both ways. Think of rapport as to know, like and trust.

Building rapport is a valuable skill you can use everywhere. You can use it to:

* build and enhance relationships

* break the ice with new work colleagues

* gain support for your ideas or proposals

Here are five simple steps to help you build rapport

1. Establish common ground.

This may sound pretty obvious, but whenever you're meeting someone new, do your best to find things you have in common. In business, the first place I would start, prior to any meeting, would be LinkedIn.

Look at the profile of the person you want to connect with. Where did they go to school and what did they study at university? Which businesses or industries have they worked in? Do you have common connections? Perhaps you share the same hobbies and interests or support the same football team?

Any common ground can help to break the ice and easily help to establish rapport. Be genuine and sincere though. 'Fake it till you make it' encapsulates all that is bad in the old sales world of slippery, slimy salespeople and it will shoot your credibility in the foot.

One of my all-time favourite words in the English dictionary is 'verisimilitude'. It means to give something the appearance of being real or true. So instead of 'fake it till you make it,' practice verisimilitude when looking for common ground.

That sounds better, doesn't it?

2. Dress to impress.

I don't mean black-tie or ballgown (unless it's that kind of occasion when you meet). Your appearance and how you dress should help you connect, not create a barrier.

As a general rule people like people who are like themselves.

Adapt a chameleon-like approach on a first meeting. What I mean is if you're meeting an engineering workshop manager in a factory environment it may be more applicable to be dressed in jeans and casual shirt than a well-tailored expensive Italian suit.

3. Show empathy.

See things from the other person's perspective, don't just meet to serve your own agenda. Consider what's happening in their world right now that might be making them happy and what could be causing them stress?

Are they more likely to be detail orientated, focused on systems and processes, or are they more outgoing, people focused and gregarious? Understanding someone's 'personality profile', how they like to give and receive information, the pace they work at, even think at, can unlock a veritable treasure chest at work and in your personal life too.

*** I have used all sorts of different profiling systems in business such as DISC, Myers Briggs and many others. Which, if any, are you familiar with? I now use**

the very best of the best with all of my coaching and mentoring clients, it's called Talent Dynamics. More than 500,000 people around the world have benefited from it too. I have used Talent Dynamics with numerous businesses to help them recruit and build their dream teams, tap into their hidden talents and unlock their true potential with accelerating productivity, performance and profits. More on this in the last chapter - (go on then, skip back there if you must, but come on back here...)

4. Match and mirror

If you're familiar with NLP you will be familiar with this term. (NLP stands for *neurolinguistic programming*, or as I like to think of it, common sense written down).

Matching and mirroring is basically when you adjust your own body language and the spoken word to reflect that the person you're talking to.

As you can imagine there could be a very obvious mismatch and therefore, a break in rapport if you speak too loudly or in a fast paced excitable tone to somebody who is more shy, reserved and introverted. The opposite is also true, of course. A fast paced creative thinker or extrovert will not feel too comfortable working at a slow pace or being bogged down with detail.

OK, maybe I owe an apology to NLP practitioners, perhaps there is a lot more to this than just common sense written down. Sorry!

5. Remember the basics

* Smile

* Look people in the eye

* Use a firm but comfortable handshake, no knuckle crashing required, no slippery wet fish handshakes acceptable either.

* Be courteous and polite, be respectful of people's time and space.

* Listen more than you speak, and really listen; don't just wait for your turn to speak.

These basic tenets form the foundation of all great communication and it is hard, if not impossible, to establish good rapport without them.

.....

Do you speak the same language as your clients?

I was speaking at a conference in Skopje, Macedonia.

As is often the case when I speak abroad, my words were being simultaneously translated into the native tongue. On this occasion there were actually two translators on hand, one to translate into Albanian and another into Macedonian. They did a fantastic job.

Without their help about half the audience would not have been able to understand the points I was making. My messages would have been pretty useless and of no real benefit to them.

Now, before any of you joke with me about my information being of little value anyway…

Here are just a couple of messages I received via LinkedIn, the day after the event. The first was from one of the Albanian delegates who was using the translation service.

'Thank you a lot. I did the 3 call concept today before I looked at my emails as you said. One of the calls resulted in a sale that paid for me to attend the event 8 times over! I will continue with calls, and come to more of your events! Thank you.'

How about this from another attendee:

'I attended Steve Clarke's seminar in Skopje. He definitely provoked me to think 'outside of the box' and to get out of my 'comfort zone' to get more sales. His ideas are simple but practical, new and refreshing, and everyone can apply them. Thanks to his motivational speech I made a client call during the seminar break and the next day the client sent an order of €800,000. Thank you Steve, sometimes we forget about the simple things. I certainly recommend it to everyone as he

is so different, so inspiring and motivating. I would love to visit some other seminar with him.'

Katerina Zecevic - Commercial Sales Director at Wabtec MZT

So back to the point. The importance of building rapport in a 'yes' culture.

I explained to the delegates about using the right language with their clients and prospects so that they too get their message across.

All too often people with technical products or services want to demonstrate how much they know by using technical talk. STOP IT! You will be losing business.

Speak in language the person you are speaking to understands (or in my case have it translated in real time). Speak at a pace and tone that they are comfortable with. Get in rapport.

Show you care, show you understand the challenge or issue the client faces. Give them a clear concise message they can easily understand. Let them know how you and/or your business can help solve their problem and relieve their pain.

Remember, people don't care how much you know, until they know how much you care.

.....

***Eureka*! Using different language increases sales!**

'I run a small group of independent opticians.

It's a stable established business with over 95% repeat clients year on year. They say yes after just one or two (nudge) letters - sounds like a dream place to be?

It's easy to be distracted by the surface sales, but analysis of the demographics of our repeat customers shows that a huge number of them are in their late 70s and over, with an ever decreasing number in their 40s.

That's not a long term secure pipeline as many of our customers are going to move on to 'another place' where they just won't need their eyes looked after!

Our repeat customers were responding to the service they had historically received but new prospects were not responding to our marketing messaging. I needed to change how we did things.
Steve quickly understood what the problem was and improved my language skills to help engage with a new audience and build rapport with them.

Our training is very technical and what are everyday terms and scenarios for us is completely alien to our prospects. I knew what they needed from a technical standpoint, but wasn't presenting them with information in a way that was easy to understand so that they could make an informed decision whether to buy from us or not.

A confused buyer never buys.

Combining this with Steve's 'upserve' philosophy, we have exceeded all goals and expectations. Sales went up 19% to give us our best ever year (in our 28 years of business) and we are attracting a significant number of new families - parents in their 40's and their children, so a good pipeline for future success.'

Gavin Rebello – Partner at Patrick & Menzies

Patrick & Menzies
INDEPENDENT OPTOMETRISTS AND OPTICIANS

Take a moment to review the way you communicate in person, in email, on your website. Are you speaking in a language that is clearly understood? Are you building rapport or putting obstacles in your way?

.....

How far can you reach?

We all have the opportunity to broaden our reach and connect with more people now more than at any other time in history. British astronaut and test pilot Major Tim Peake spent six months in 2016 living on board the International

Space Station. Whilst orbiting the Earth once every 92 minutes at a speed of over 17,000 mph (that's about 5 miles per second), he was able to conduct interviews with the world's media and bring science lessons to hundreds of thousands of children back home. He has a huge following on social media including over 1 million Twitter followers. That's reach!

Sports personalities and A-list celebrities have such reach and influence that it leaves all of the big-brand names salivating as they clamber for endorsements. Footballer Cristiano Ronaldo has a staggering 45 million followers on Twitter alone!

But you don't need to be a celebrity to create or benefit from the reach made available to us all through the Internet and social media as proven by Chewbacca's mum.

On May 19, 2016, 37-year-old mother of two Candace Payne, filmed herself laughing like crazy while wearing a Star Wars Chewbacca mask. She posted a four-minute video on Facebook with a description 'it's the simple joys in life' in which she explained that the toy mask was hers, not her kids. She had bought it for herself. She proceeded to demonstrate how the mask worked as she wept with laughter.

Due to her infectious laughter, people couldn't resist sharing the video with their friends. Within five days the video had more than 140 million views on Facebook making it the most viewed live video of all time. The toy mask sold out at every online retailer.

Chewbacca mum mania kicked into gear as Candace was invited onto the *Late Late Show* with James Corden and Facebook headquarters with Mark Zuckerberg. She was being interviewed by every TV station and showered with gifts from various manufacturers and corporates all eager to get in on the action.

If anyone had suggested to you that for business or personal purposes what you really needed was a global TV network to broaden your reach you'd have thought they were barking mad. Today that's precisely what we all have at our fingertips through our smartphones, tablets and laptops. And the cost to use these global platforms? Practically nothing other than a little imagination and creativity.

The kind of global reach and viral video sensation that I just described is utopia, but you don't need this kind of extreme result to have a huge impact on your life or your business.

Think about the market you want to reach in order to achieve your goals and you may be surprised how broad the reach can become when you throw a pebble into the pond and the ripples start to spread.

However, size isn't everything!

Focus on what you want to achieve and don't get hung up on technology. It's not about technology, it's about reaching people. It's about conversations not publications. It's about a return on engagement!

In order to get traction your video or your message needs to be relevant, helpful, unique, interesting, funny or controversial or maybe even the full set.

.....

Technology. It's all Greek to me

Well, a mix of Greek, English and Kiwi in fact. Allow me to explain.

It was a first for me when I, an Englishman, an Essex boy in fact, addressed a conference of several hundred people in Athens, Greece, whilst staying in a beautiful house high above a Marlborough vineyard in New Zealand overlooking the Tasman Sea.

It was a speaking engagement for an annual sales management forum that I was approached to do several months previously. Initially I was very excited to receive the enquiry, then all at once disappointed to find that it clashed with my trip to Australia and New Zealand. Reluctantly, I turned down the work.

I was even considering cutting short my visit to New Zealand as I read over the proposed agenda that looked like it would now go on without me.

Then I read item number 3 on the agenda:

3. How can we reduce the cost of sales?

Then item number 4:

4. How can we increase our sales on the global stage during tough economic times?

Ping! The light bulb came on. I had a Eureka moment!

I quickly crafted an email to the event organiser and hit 'send' in the hope I could reverse my previous decision and still be invited to take part.

In the email I pointed out that I could still speak at the conference as requested, but with a difference: I would do it remotely via Skype. This would address and demonstrate both items 3 and 4 on their agenda. Brilliant, or so I thought.

Back came the reply; thanks, but we've tried a live Skype call in the past, it didn't work.

So what now? That's it, decision made?

Tried it before. Does that mean it couldn't or wouldn't work in future? No. Things change, technology moves on.

So, instead of another email, I did what I suggest to people all the time. **I picked up the phone.** The organiser in Greece wasn't expecting that!

After initial introductions, I politely asked how could they have points 3 and 4 on the agenda and not try to demonstrate how to achieve what they're asking?

I explained how much things have changed and how I use Skype all the time for coaching calls, then I offered my back up plan too. I'd record a piece to camera addressing the questions they would ask me live. If technology bombed on the day, flick the switch and run plan B. They can even have the video to circulate after the event to all the delegates. (That's the video which is loaded with all my contact info so I can work on building future relationships).

I had engaged. We were in rapport, I'd removed the pain. We created a 'yes!' They agreed.

The call went without any hitches and I was even able to take live questions from the audience. In summing up, the host thanked me and then asked if I'd be happy to appear in person at their conference next year as there was clearly lots more to share. Great result all round.

What can you take from this?

We need to think outside the box. Look for alternative and creative solutions for our clients if we want business and not excuses for why you didn't get to 'yes'.

Getting to 'yes' means not just taking no for an answer, it may also need further exploration and explanation.

Pick up the phone and talk to people, never rely only on emails. Learn to embrace technology, it can massively broaden your reach!

As proven by an Englishman who was actually in New Zealand when he spoke at a conference in Athens and was awarded speaker of the conference, without actually being there!

'I am really happy that we decided to try something new and have you in our conference using Skype for a live interview. I am sorry only for one thing – something our delegates agree with too: we should have more time to profit from your expertise in sales, and the way you present new trends in such a simple and clear way! Next time we will have the pleasure to welcome you in Athens, as our keynote speaker.'

Xenia Mantziori – Boussias Communications – Athens.

.....

Lessons from an Athens taxi driver.

A year later I was invited back to speak in person. The event organiser kindly had a chauffeur collect me at the airport.

As we chatted during the journey I was reminded, in no uncertain terms by my driver, what a desperate time many Greeks were experiencing. Massive unemployment, pitifully low minimum wages of those lucky enough to have a job. They were deep into a severe financial 'crisis' and were just two days from a general election, tough times for Greeks no doubt and a tough gig for a business growth speaker too!

I was all geared up to share hints, tips and strategies to boost sales and profits. My keynote was entitled: 'Champagne results on a beer budget'. It was full of low cost and no cost solutions to boosting sales. It was as requested by the organizer, but how could I do this without belittling their massive challenges? What could I share that would not sound arrogant or patronising? How could I ensure that I build rapport with the audience and kept my client happy?

Arriving a day ahead of the conference I decided to visit the sights of Athens taking in not only it's spectacular history, but seeking fresh inspiration for my keynote too.

"Head towards the city centre," said the hotel concierge. "Cross the road, take the second road on the right, walk about 100 yards and you'll reach the Metro. It's just six stops and only costs 1.20 Euro," he explained.

Quick and cheap, that's what he was thinking. Times of austerity and cut backs.

At that moment I was a tourist. What did I want? I wanted sight-seeing. He was suggesting I head underground. What would I see?

I did as he suggested, just in case it was like no other metro in the world, and what did I see? A crowded train, lots of people and a dark tunnel, but he was right, it was cheap. However, it failed to meet my needs and wants.

Do you listen to what your boss, or your clients and prospects actually want? Or do you make suggestions and proposals based on certain assumptions?

I took a couple of taxis after the underground experience, visiting the early Olympic Stadium and other spectacular ancient buildings around the city. It was great to be above ground and enjoy the sights and sounds of a beautiful, bustling city, but again, each driver was full of doom and gloom.

Moan, groan – 4 euros, thanks. Moan, complain - 4 euros, thanks and then to my great fortune I hailed a taxi driven by George.

He welcomed me with a smile. I asked if he could take me to the Acropolis. We set off on our way. As he drove we engaged in conversation.

“Tough right now, isn’t it?” I said with a sigh having been conditioned with negativity since arriving in town.

“For sure, it’s tough, but what’s easier to change? The state of the economy or our attitude towards it?” he said.

Wow!

That’s the kind of stuff I tell people all the time, now George was my teacher. I loved his attitude.

He continued…

“How long are you visiting for? Only the Acropolis won’t look at its best at this time of day; if you’re tight on time you might be better to visit this place or that and come back to the Acropolis just after lunch,” he explained.

(I can't remember the names of the places he mentioned, but at this point I was more focused on the fact that he was focused on me, my wants and needs and was potentially 'up selling', or 'up serving', me better that anyone else I'd met).

"Great idea. How would I get to all these places?" I asked.

He explained that there are buses and trains, if I could work out which ones to get. Or I could take different taxis from place to place.

He'd quickly become my trusted advisor.

"Could you take me please, George?" I asked.

Well, surprise, surprise, he could and for 40 euros he would turn the meter off and stick with me all morning and show me around. He actually turned a 4 euro taxi ride into 60 euros including a tip by the time we'd done.

How are you 'up-serving' your clients?

He was brilliant. We drove to the coast and chatted over a coffee. George explained how he helped his wife get a job in nursing which she's now had for eight years. He did this after a chance conversation with a doctor, another customer in his cab.

Chance? No. After a conversation he engaged in and listened carefully to. Then took action; he called the doctor as requested once his wife was qualified. Not once, but several times until he reached him.

How persistent are you with your follow up?

When we reached the Acropolis I asked him to park up and join me.

He shared yet more wisdom.

“Look at the structure of the building,” he said.

“There are many columns supporting the roof. Not one, but many, that’s how we need to be in business and in society. We need many levels of support.”

Brilliant, thanks to George, my talk was coming together.

He finally pointed out another lesson for us all in a busy market square. Vendors had stalls crammed with all manner of items: everything for anyone, pile them high and sell them cheap. Much the same stuff on every stall, all they could do was compete on price.

Then we turned into a quieter road and George pointed to a shop window. The shop sold olive oil, but these people don’t sell the low end to every household. They sell only high end, beautifully packaged, very fine olive oil and to clients from all over the world that want the best. What crisis? There is no crisis!

When times are challenging sell differently, sell to someone different or sell something different. Don’t just keep doing the same as everyone else and hoping for better results.

Just think of how many ways each of George's stories applies to your job or your business.

As I took to the stage my first slide was from my original talk: 'Champagne results on a beer budget'.

I explained how inappropriate I felt that would be given the way things were in their country at that time. I went on to explain that I had an amazing day of sight-seeing. So instead of my planned talk, I'd like to share a new talk and I clicked the remote control to reveal my new title: 'Sales lessons from an Athens taxi driver'. They cheered and gave me a huge round of applause.

I changed my entire talk, although I delivered the same messages, but through a new hero in my story, one of their own: George the taxi driver. **Thanks to him I was able to engage with the audience and build great rapport.**

Here's the feedback I got from the organiser on this second trip:

'*The delegates were more than pleased to hear your very inspirational speech! It was the highest rated talk of all 20 speakers at the conference! We will work together again in our future events!*'

Ξένια Μαντζιώρη

Διευθύντρια Σύνταξης Σελφ Σέρβις

Boussias Communications

The only thing George didn't thank me for was that I gave the audience his mobile number and asked that they text him to say thanks for the lessons.

He did send me a text to say thanks, but I'd rather be driving for paying customers than spending all day reading texts!

.....

Stand out from the crowd

Broaden your **reach** if you're looking for work or wanting to stand out from the crowd.

Here are just two examples of people that have dared to be different, using traditional 'ish' methods and leveraging technology.

It's tough out there to find work for many people, no doubt, but what good does bitching and moaning about it do?

I love this man. Meet Adam Pacitti. Having applied for over 250 jobs with no luck, he didn't roll over and play dead. He took massive action.

Adam, an unemployed graduate spent his last £500 on a billboard advertisement practically begging for a job. He then directed would-be employers to his website. Simple as that. He received more than 100 job offers and his advert went viral thanks to social media.

His campaign paid off too. He landed a job with a top media firm in London. Delighted with his new 'employed' status what did Mr Pacitti splash out on with his first pay packet? Another huge billboard in Shoreditch, London; this time just to say thanks.

Whatever your business or whatever you want in a job, get off your backside, stop complaining and do something about it.

.....

Let's find James a job

More recently a good friend of mine and fellow speaker, Richard McCann, posted a fabulous video using Facebook Live. (Live video streaming with **global reach** and all for free!)

He'd bumped into a young man called James Durkan outside of London's Kings Cross station early in the morning of the 29th June 2016.

James was holding a message, written in green felt pen onto a large scrap of cardboard, which he held aloft for all the commuters passing him to see. It read:

"I HAVE HIGH FUNCTIONING AUTISM. PLEASE HELP ME FIND A JOB, SO I CAN BE NORMAL LIKE YOU."

Richard was intrigued, he's also got a heart the size of a double decker bus, so he stopped and spoke with James to understand his story and see if he could help in any way.

It transpired that James arrived early that morning from his hometown of Portsmouth (when I say hometown in reality it was his 'homeless' town he was living his life surfing sofas with friends). He had decided that London could provide him with the opportunity he was seeking, so he did something about it.

He had been employed by a global engineering company and was doing a diploma in engineering. James had lost his job for visiting a country on holiday that was on a 'do not visit list' according to his employer. James didn't know until he suffered the consequences.

Determined to see if he could help, Richard interviewed James using Facebook live on his iPhone outside of King's Cross station.

James gave an absolutely brilliant interview, despite his protestations about a lack of confidence in talking to people. He explained that ideally, he was looking for another opportunity in engineering and he would travel anywhere and relocate anywhere if it resulted in the right opportunity.

First dozens, then hundreds of people watched the video and cheered James on. The last time I checked this Facebook live video had been viewed 106,010 times.

Thanks to the almost unfathomable reach delivered through social media to the hands, offices and homes of us all, thousands of people watched the video and job offers started appearing.

On Thursday 7th July James accepted a new job. On Monday 11th July (12 days after he had met Richard) he started work!

He took action, he stood out. Richard took the trouble to explore and offer help. A massive team effort ensued through the reach of social media and James can now be NORMAL like the rest of us. Whatever that is! Well done all.

Eureka moments in the R of EUREKA

*** Follow the five simple steps to building rapport**

*** Do you speak the same language as the people you want to build rapport with?**

*** People don't care how much you know, until they know how much you care**

*** How far can you reach?**

*** Technology - it's all Greek to me**

*** Lessons from an Athens taxi driver**

*** Stand out from the crowd**

*** Let's find James a job**

Take time to reflect on this. Who do you want to reach and why?

It's a fact that our possible reach today totally exceeds the wildest dreams of our potential reach just a few years ago.

How can you leverage the contacts you have and increase your reach?

Coming up next in helping you create and live your life in a culture of 'yes'. The second E in EUREKA - and this stands for Endurance.

Chapter 5

EUREKA

Endurance

'It always seems impossible until it's done.' Nelson Mandela

Staying the course is as much about mental strength as physical fitness.

I'm so proud to say that in 2012, the London Olympic year, my wife Susanne completed her first London Marathon. She's now run it four times and raised lots of money for charity in the process.

Whilst her time may have been a way off the winner it was an amazing accomplishment for her, as indeed it is for everyone that puts themselves through such a demanding event. I'm a keen sportsman, but I've never been keen on distance running. I've always been fine with short bursts, but lacked the mental and physical strength required for endurance sports, or so I thought.

Susanne explained to me that training and getting fit for the marathon was not that different to training and succeeding in business. She pointed out all the things I do to help business owners with their sales and marketing efforts. How without my support as their business coach and mentor people often see the road ahead of them as an impossible challenge.

What she then went on to explain made a lot of sense to me.

'It's about learning certain techniques and having a strategy.'

OK, I can relate to that.

'It's about not over stretching yourself, but pacing yourself.'

Yep, I get this too.

'It's about having a support network, a good trainer to help you break things down into manageable chunks, having measurable milestones. Not looking at an almost insurmountable 26.2 miles, but looking ahead to reach the corner of the street, the next lamp post or street sign – small milestones. These all add up. However, to achieve the end goal you need to get out of your comfort zone and stretch yourself.'

All of these are things I've told my children growing up and it's what I tell my business clients too.

Spurred on by my wife's enthusiasm and encouragement I recently took to the streets myself.

I'd also loaded an app onto my iPhone. The music played and I ran to the beat, (not too loud and only one ear piece in so I could easily hear what else was going on around me before I take a bashing from the health and safety police) the app kept track of my performance too. I can't tell you how excited I got when Paula Radcliffe, yep Paula herself, announced over my headphones that I'd just completed my first and fastest mile and the virtual crowd cheered me on. There was my support and encouragement, the bounce came back into my stride.

This is just the same for so many people in business. Day in, day out pounding the metaphorical streets, mile after mile with no measurable milestones, nobody to cheer you on, nobody to help with your strategy, nobody to pick you up when you stumble, no finish line or medal in sight, it will and it can wear you out.

What does your support network look like? How strong is your team? How good is your trainer and coach?

Running a marathon, just like running a business requires mental strength as much as it does physical fitness. Each part of the marathon and every business has its own mental challenges. Baby steps and encouragement will win through.

Here are some tips from Susanne on how to maintain your focus and win the mental battles throughout the marathon. Can you spot the similarities in business?

Susanne's tips for running your marathon

Pace yourself. When you start your marathon, you'll feel strong and confident, but you must keep telling yourself to hold back and conserve some energy.

Run your own race. Don't be worried if you see a lot of people passing you. Remember the tortoise and the hare? They may be starting out way too fast, so you can catch them later at your pace.

Break it up. Start breaking up the race into smaller segments. It will make the distance feel more manageable and you will notice the small wins along the way.

Keep your eye on the prize. Your mental toughness will really start to be tested during these miles. Don't give in to periods of self-doubt and discomfort. Think about how hard you've worked and how rewarding it will be to complete your marathon.

Celebrate along the way. Continue to break up the course, mile by mile. Celebrate your achievements along the way, don't lose sight of how well you're doing and listen to the crowds cheering you on.

.....

Cancun - Can help

Kseniya Kreger, a Russian client, had booked me to speak at her company's conference in Cancun, Mexico. On day one I delivered a leadership and teamwork training for a hundred of the company's top leaders and on day two a motivational and sales training for over 600 delegates.

It was a fantastic, well organised event with a lively and enthusiastic audience. My session on day two ended in rapturous applause and a standing ovation. The applause and cheers for me on day three were almost as loud and I wasn't even there and it wasn't because I wasn't there that they cheered either! Here's what happened:

At the time I was in training for my first official 10km run. After the long flight from London to Cancun I was in need of some exercise to wake me up and get the blood pumping in order to be at my best for the audience. I put my running gear on, activated my running app and set off.

The humidity was high, I was tired and it was tough. I started out slowly and took it at my own pace, but it honestly felt like someone had put lead weights into my running shoes. By the time I reached 3km I felt exhausted. I pushed on at a steady pace, taking some of Susanne's early running advice and picking out lampposts and buildings ahead of me setting them as small milestones and it helped, a little.

By 6km I was done. I felt exhausted and didn't want to pick up any injuries as the next day I had to be on stage and on top of my game. I stopped.

Feeling the effects of jetlag I was up at silly o'clock on the first day of the conference. I decided I needed to wake myself up. On with my running shoes, shorts and t-shirt and back to the streets I went with 10km in my sights. I had never run in such humidity and again found it quite a struggle. This time I made it to 6km and called it a day.

The exercise did the trick. I felt awake and alert and as a result delivered a great session according to the feedback from Kseniya and her leadership team on day one.

Day two of the conference was a big one. 600 people waiting to be educated and motivated. Whether I'm speaking to 6, 60 or 600 people I always want to bring my A game. So you guessed it, prior to the conference I was back pounding the streets again to energise myself.

As I spoke, my words were being translated into Spanish and then further translated into 23 other languages! Prior to the start of the conference I had spent some time with the interpreters to check they understood the intention and meaning of my talk. They were brilliant and picked up everything in my messages.

During my talk I made reference to the fact that their business, like every other one that I know, has a high reliance on endurance. I explained how they should take their business at their pace, set milestones and celebrate success.

I decided to use my running analogy to explain what I meant. They all understood. Getting to 'yes' and creating a 'yes' culture was about running their own race, setting their own goals, working in pursuit of them and measuring their success along the way.

I also explained that in the absence of a physical trainer or training team, how we all have voices in our head. If you're thinking to yourself now 'I don't have voices in my head.' That's the one I'm talking about! They are the voices of either our inner critic or inner coach. They will cheer you on or hold you back in all areas of your life.

The inner critic will tell you 'you can't, you're not good enough, who do you think you are?' Whilst your inner coach will cheer you on with a 'yes you can, go for it, well done!'

I had incorporated a screenshot from my running app into my presentation. I explained that I set out with the intention of running 10km, but had barely made it halfway. On screen they could see the route of my 6km run. Was that a failure? No, it was just the outcome of the day, providing I listen to my inner coach and my inner cheerleader not my inner critic.

I continued my story.
"Determined to reach my 10km goal I set out before most of you were up for your breakfast on this, the second day of the conference. It was hot, it was humid, it was tough, but I had a goal, I had great determination."

Then I questioned the audience.

"Do you have firm goals? Do you have belief in your ability?"

"Yes," came the resounding reply from the audience in unison.

"Do you really? Do you honestly believe that you can achieve whatever you set out to do?"

"YES!" they cheered like a well-lead and excited audience.

Then I popped up the screen shot of my run that morning.

"I only managed 6km. I failed to achieve my goal," I said.

"No," they shouted back.

I handed a mic to a member of the audience who was very animated.

"You didn't fail. You got out there, you did your best, you did better than before, keep going, next time or the time after that. You'll get to your 10km. Believe you can, you have to believe you can. Don't feel bad, feel proud, feel good, we are all behind you," and 600 people cheered and clapped!

I had only used my running analogy to emphasise my message of setting big goals and celebrating smaller milestones along the way. I wanted them to be fully aware of the voices we all have in our heads.

Which voice dominates that space in your head? Your inner critic or your inner coach?

In developing and embedding a 'yes' culture in your life, at work and play, it's imperative that you recognise your critic and your coach and develop the skills of tuning them in and tuning them out.

The conference continued into day three, but with the exception of my appearance at the gala dinner that evening, my official work was all done.

Early that morning there was a voice in my head telling me to rollover and go back to sleep.

'You're tired, it's already hot outside. You're not going to get to 10km anyway rollover, take the day off.' Which voice was this? No prize for guessing.

Then my inner coach piped up.

'Come on, get up, you can do it. Even if you get to 5,6 or 7km it will make you feel good. Do it for the delegates. You told them all about grit and determination, you told them about the importance of having goals, don't let them down. Get out of bed you lazy sod, get your shoes on and get at it.'

My inner coach can be pretty direct and even harsh sometimes! So I was up and at it. The first 2km felt great. From 3 to 5km I began to feel the heat, but pushed on. At 6km my inner critic was telling me to quit. Suddenly he seemed to find a couple of mates out of nowhere! Various voices were telling me to stop, pack it in. You're going to damage your knees, your back is going to ache, then the killer blow. A dark little voice seemed to whisper in my ear;

'Don't worry, no one will know if you just call it a day. No need to even tell them you came out for a run, that way you can't fail. Heck, just tell them you did it, they'll will be none the wiser.' The dirty rotten cheat!

If my inner critic could call on his mates, then so too could my coach. I was able to visualise the 600 strong audience that genuinely cheered me on the day before and congratulated me on my efforts. A massive team of virtual cheerleaders in my head gave me a new spring in my step as I clocked up the kilometres. Eight and nine were tough. With the conference centre just half a kilometre away it marked the finish line of my 10km run. The voices in my head cheered me on as the app on my phone announced:

'Distance completed - 10 km!'

After a cool down and a shower I sent Kseniya a screen shot of the map of my run and explained how I couldn't have achieved my goal without the support of all her people cheering me on in my head, I meant it. Unbeknown to me, Kseniya added that as a slide to her presentation that morning. That's when I got a massive cheer and loud applause and I wasn't even in the room.

I believe in those few days I demonstrated a couple of key points very clearly through my running. One about setting clear goals, but also knowing that often achieving your goals is more about endurance than a sprint. But the key learning has to be the acceptance that we all have voices in our heads.

Learn to listen to your inner coach if you want to create and embed a 'yes' culture in your life.

.....

WTF?!

WTF, it's probably not what you're thinking!

WTF for me is - Where's The Focus?

In the Cancun story I mentioned the importance of goals. They give you focus.

Imagine a game of football without goalposts. 22 players on the pitch, all chasing a ball, tackling each other, but not knowing what to do with the ball when they get it. They don't know what they're shooting for and there's no way of tracking the progress of the game.

Golf without a flag and the hole? Which club would you select, which direction would you aim in?

Both examples sound rather crazy, but you get my point.

I'm amazed by how many people have no focus or strategy for getting what they want out of their life or their business. I know plenty of people in the business world who actually spend more time and effort planning their summer holiday than they do truly planning their business or what they want out of life.

Where's your focus? Remember this:

'Where your focus goes your energy flows'.

I'm a big believer in having personal and business goals. I set goals in all areas of my life to keep me focused and help maintain momentum. If we're not growing, developing and moving forwards there's only one place we are headed and that's south!

I don't mean that you can't be happy and content with what you have, we should all spend time reflecting and counting our blessings. However, I'm a huge fan of personal growth and business development and from me, in the business world, they can often go hand in hand.

I'm not a believer of the popular phrase 'you can't teach an old dog new tricks.' If the old dog wants to learn and focuses time, effort and energy amazing things can be achieved. The key word in that last sentence is 'want'. For a goal to be effective you have to own it, you have to want it, you have to be able to visualise the end result. Do you have to know how to achieve the goal? Absolutely not.

Whilst watching infomercials on late-night television when I lived and worked in America I was first exposed to the giant that is Tony Robbins. He is an absolute legend in the world of personal development and may already be known to you. I spent a lot of the time on road trips driving across the United States with Tony Robbins for company via his CDs.

On one of my trips I tried to introduce a relative who was out visiting with us to the teachings of Mr Robbins. The problem was he didn't really want to see any change. I found it difficult to comprehend, but discovered over time that constantly being the victim worked for him.

All very American and full of hype was how he described it. In fact he even referred to it as brainwashing. I'd actually agree with two out of three of those sentiments. It is very American and it is kind of brainwashing, but in a good way on both counts. Is it hype? Definitely not. Reframing your thought patterns and choosing to create positive outcomes are all within our grasp.

There are hundreds of books written on this one subject alone. I don't want to turn this book into a goal setting masterclass, there are plenty of people equipped better than me to help you on this particular subject. I reference this only

to reinforce that creating a 'yes' culture is very much about having you, and the people within your organization, focused on positive, chosen outcomes and that designing your life and the business you want is within your grasp.
Having great big lofty goals, may seem unattainable when you set them, but they also become exciting, motivating, challenging and incredibly rewarding along the way. When you achieve them they are even better. What great goals do is give you focus and motivation.

Some people set their sights very low. How exciting is it to shoot for 'mediocrity'? I remember one of the only times I caught a glimpse of the TV soap *Eastenders*. I heard a father giving his son this gem for advice: "Expect the worst my son, that way you'll never be disappointed."

Oh my god! What a set up for a miserable existence! Imagine spending every day expecting the worst. Guess what's coming their way? Where your focus goes your energy flows. At a time when I really needed to refocus my attention and reset some goals it just happened that Tony Robbins was coming to the UK with his signature 'Unleash the power within' event. I signed up without hesitation. I doubt many avid viewers of *Eastenders* did.

On the opening day of the four-day event the crowds began to gather. There were clearly hundreds of Tony Robbins junkies in attendance all hugging and high-fiving like there was no tomorrow.

The second the auditorium doors opened, the crowds poured in. Music was belting out, lights were flashing, people were dancing in the aisles. They had a full professional dance troupe on stage and then the man himself appeared gyrating to the music and clapping his ridiculously oversized hands and smiling to reveal teeth that are almost as big as me!

My first thought: 'Oh my God, what had I let myself in for? I should have stayed at home and caught up with *Eastenders* (no, it wasn't quite that bad).'

As the music subsided he invited us to go and hug three people we'd never met before.

My second thought was: 'Oh my God, how do I get out of here?'

I had listened to his CDs, I understood the power of what he teaches first hand. I can attribute a lot of the success that I had with my business in America to applying what I learnt from his CDs. I'd also invested a substantial amount of money on a four-day event. I decided to not be 'quite so British' and threw myself into it.

By the end of the first day I completed the fire walk. In fact, it was getting on for 2 o'clock in the morning when 3000 delegates left the conference hall and moved as one to the car park where the fire pits had been prepared with red-hot embers.

Not one person burnt their feet. It's not something I need to repeat nor is it something I want to spend more time on here as I fear that a few of you may already be thinking I've lost the plot. What I took from the fire walk was the metaphor that if you put your mind to it you can achieve things you never would have thought were possible.

I set a number of goals over the course of that weekend; some relatively small, some positively life changing. I quit smoking, changed my diet, lost weight and improved my fitness. All good.
One of the biggest goals I set myself was to retire at the age of 45! I had no idea how I was going achieve this. It was certainly a lofty goal.

At that point in time I had just gone through a costly divorce. I had parted with my marital home and all the savings I had in the world. I was living in a small house with a hundred percent mortgage and I had my name on a business overdraft to the tune of £1/2 million. I wasn't just starting from ground zero I was already in a great big hole.

What I had was a business with promise, lots of energy and enthusiasm and a clearly written goal: to retire at the age of 45.

In order to achieve your goals I believe you not only need to visualise them as being real and true and see yourself having achieved them, see yourself in the moment, but you must clearly write them down.

I delivered a talk once in India and we got onto the subject of goal setting. A member of the audience told me he agreed entirely with the importance of committing to your goals in writing. What he said I loved:

'If you can think it you must ink it.'

Having created a vision for myself of early retirement I made sure that every day in some way I was taking action and moving closer inch by inch. When I set my goal, retirement was five years off. It wasn't a sprint it was an endurance event.

It gave me focus when it came to account management and business growth. It helped me make decisions on hiring the right team members who were also focused on growth. It helped me make a decision on parting with some equity in order to get the right team on board all pulling in the same direction.

Just two years later my business partner and I found ourselves in a meeting at the Belfry Golf Club in Birmingham with our biggest competitor at the time (double our size) with a view to selling them our business. The sale would have been substantial, and yet it wouldn't have put me in a position where I'd achieve my goal and be able to retire, mortgage free, debt free with cash in the bank.

I detected early in the conversation that in fact we may be playing the wrong game and called for a comfort break. I discussed with my business partner what I'd picked up on during conversation. I believed that rather than buyers the people we were sitting with could actually be sellers. We agreed to change tack and went back to the table with a different approach.

It transpired that our hunch was correct. After a brief period of due diligence we were able to raise finance and complete a 'David and Goliath' style takeover. This put us in a very clear market leading position with a huge uplift in turnover and through the economy of scale also increased our bottom line profit substantially.

We successfully grew the company year-on-year, becoming number 87 on the Times top 100 fastest growing SMEs list in the UK.

.....

September 30th - mark that in your diary.

It's my birthday. OK, a cheap shot, but if I keep telling people I may see more cards on the day!

Here's the relevance.

My goal was to retire at the age of 45.

We had now found ourselves a buyer. We had racked up huge legal and accounting fees, gone through months of extensive due diligence and negotiations and on September 29th, whilst I was still 45, we were locked in offices in London with lawyers and accountants from both sides as we tried to thrash out the final paperwork in order that we could complete the sale.

By the time we reached 4.30pm one of the lawyers from the other side suggested, "Gentleman, we're all getting rather fractious, what do you say that we adjourn until tomorrow?"

My goal was clearly written down! Today I'm 45, tomorrow I will be 46, that meant I would miss my goal if we adjourned. What chance do you think they had of getting out of the room?

Absolutely zero!

My partner and I left them to it. We took off to put on expenses the last meal we could on the company whilst we owned it before heading back to complete the sale.
Finally, at 11.30pm on 29 September we signed over the business to the new owners. I had achieved my great big lofty goal with half an hour to spare. I retired at 45… just!

The irony is that I'm now busier than I think I've ever been, so much for retirement! I did actually have a couple of years off; I travelled a lot, had a great time, but my life lacked purpose. I would call my friends to see who was available for a game of golf. 'Sod off Clarkie, I've got work to do,' was invariably the response. Playing golf with 75-year-old men wasn't how I really pictured retirement.

Whilst my goal was written down and clearly stated, I hadn't defined what retirement for me really looked like. I now know this is it: having the time and energy to help others achieve their goals.

When you do what you truly love doing and do it with purpose and passion you never actually work another day in your life.

.....

What are you aiming for - where are you heading?

As a coach and mentor I often get called upon by business owners and companies because sales targets are not being met.

I'm amazed at the amount of people I speak to, not just start-ups, but business people who own substantial, even international businesses that don't have a clear, simple, written plan, with clear goals and objectives.

I don't mean a 30-page b***s*** thing you prepared for the bank and then put in your bottom drawer and never look at it again. That's not the kind of plan I'm talking about.

Do you know where you're heading? Where is your focus?

What I often find in business is that the boss has the vision and the goals in his or her head, but has failed to share that vision with their team in a way that people know what actions to take and what direction to head in. There may even be a vision statement hanging in reception. Has anyone read it? Can anyone that has read it remember what it says? I doubt it.

Do you use a sat nav in the car?

Maybe like me, you'd now be so lost without your sat nav in the car. So set one in your life, set one for your business and set one for your team.

Here are the basic elements of the *Eureka* sat nav, and the key to this is working in small chunks or bullet points, this is a one or at the most a two page plan. A living breathing document that will help you make decisions on the direction to take on this endurance trip.

Vision
Long term goals and milestones 5 - 10 years
Mid term goals and milestones 3 - 5 years

Short term goals and milestones 1 year
90 day milestones
Top three challenges

Vision and values

Successful business owners and entrepreneurs have a clear vision for what they are building, the direction they are heading in and they have the ability to communicate this clearly and concisely to their teams and the people they chose to surround themselves with. It would be true to say that it's what attracts the right people to the business.

Visionaries have the ability to get everyone to see where the business is going and to buy into how it's going to happen. It sounds simple, but it's not.

Are your staff, or your virtual team if you outsource, all heading and pulling in the same direction? Some probably think they know best, some are coasting along, or coming along for the ride. There might be others that hide in the system just waiting for pay day.

If we were to ask individual employees in your business what the company's vision is, would they know? How about the management team? Without a clearly defined and written vision for the business it's open to various individual interpretations. If you work for a business, or you're applying for a job, check out their vision.

The clearer your vision the more likely you are to achieve it. I had to retire at 45, it was clear, concise and written down.

What are you doing and why? Imagine being up in a helicopter looking down at the ground. That's what I want you to do with your business so that you can get a 3D view of your business. Where are you going and when?
Values: what are the principles that you won't compromise?

I used to struggle with the idea of values. It all sounded too fluffy for me, then I realised how vital they are for a business to operate smoothly and effectively. It helped me to understand that people in an organisation must be aligned with the company values in order for things to run smoothly and for the team to gel.

Hire attitude, teach skills.

When you hire on a CV based on skills but then find the person doesn't fit after a period with the company, pound to a penny, it's because their values are out of sync with the company's.

So what are your values? What do you stand for or put another way, what won't you stand for? What won't you put up with?

Here's when the penny dropped for me. Here's when I got 'values'. Please bear with me on this: suspend reality for a moment, if you could fire someone from your business for any reason and HR couldn't touch you for it, what would those reasons be?

Make a list. Mine would include:- stealing, lacklustre performance, being boring, unreliable, no excitement or enthusiasm... go on make a list.

Now add the flip side of each word that p***** you off; that would be your value.

So from my list above, my values would be: Honesty, enthusiasm, fun, reliability, commitment.

Get the picture? OK, list out the things you'd fire someone for; no holds barred, this is your list. Next consider the opposite of each word. Some you will see can actually end up meaning the same thing. Whittle the hire list down to the most important ones. These, as a starting point, are your values.

Fire Hire

ENDURANCE

Once you feel right with them, they are set in stone. Remember these are your core values, your principles, you will not compromise them, you can't take the Groucho Marx approach and succeed.

***'Those are my principles, and if you don't like them... well, I have others.'* Groucho Marx**

Long term goal

(This will vary depending on your situation, industry or sector). It could be 3, 5, 10 years. What do you want to have achieved within that time frame? List 6 key objectives. For example, number of locations, number of clients, awards to have won.

Medium term

3-5 years:

What do you want to have achieved within this time frame? List 6 key objectives that will move you closer to your longer term goals. Again, measurable activity, not just sales figures. Actions deliver results.

Short term

1 year:

What do you want to have achieved within that this time frame? List 6 key objectives that will move you closer to your medium term goals. Again, measurable activity, not just sales figures. Actions deliver results.

90 day milestones

List 6 things you must achieve in 90 days that will move you closer to your mid-term goals. Perhaps launch a website, deliver x number of presentations, write a book. They must be key milestones that you can focus on that will move you closer to the mid-term and long term goals.

Issues and challenges
Consider the issues and challenges you face in hitting your various milestones. Is it one of manpower, skill set or cash? List them and figure out the top three that could cause a blockage in the first 90 days.

.....

Find a way - don't find an excuse

A really simple and highly effective brainstorming tool to help find solutions to challenges is the Questions Polygon Brainstorm the challenge or idea in a clockwise direction. If it's not working rework in an anticlockwise direction until you flush out a solution.

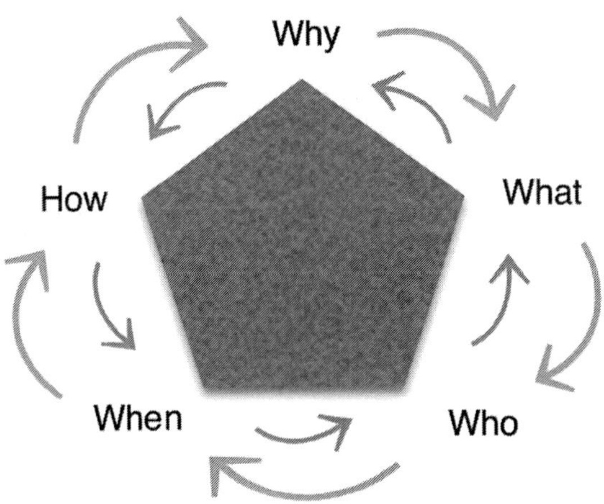

All of these questions are best answered naturally by different profiles of people. Remember I mentioned Talent Dynamics profiles? A creative person with what's known as

Dynamo energy tend to ask 'what' questions. Whilst Blaze energy people are more outgoing, people orientated and tend to ask the 'who' questions.

Please - email or call me and I will happily explain more and even provide you with a profile of your own so you get to understand the awesome power of Talent Dynamics. There's more information in the last chapter too.

.....

Remember, this fits onto a one or two page plan. I use this with individuals, small businesses and divisions within large corporations. Keeping it simple is the key. Then it's all down to attitude and action. **WTF!?!**

Keeping with the motoring theme started by the use of a sat nav, here is a questionnaire that will deliver a sensory check for you. I call it an **MOT** (Moment Of Truth).

Score each question from 0-5. Circle one number per question. Zero being, we don't have, use or even understand the statement. Five being we have or are doing precisely what you've stated. At the end total the score to give your current reality, your 'Moment Of Truth'. There are no right or wrong answers!

1: We have a crystal clear **vision** in writing for the business and it's been communicated and shared with everyone in the business.

0 1 2 3 4 5

2: Our core **values** are clear and they are in writing. We hire and fire based on them. We also use them for reviews, recognition and rewards. Suppliers are also selected to ensure they are aligned with our values.

0 1 2 3 4 5

3: Our core business niche is clear and defined in writing.

0 1 2 3 4 5

4: Our short, medium and long term goals are clear and have been communicated to everyone in the business.

0 1 2 3 4 5

5: Our target market is clearly defined, and our sales and marketing efforts are specifically focused on it.

0 1 2 3 4 5

6: Our ID (irresistible difference) is clear, and all of our sales and marketing efforts communicate our uniqueness.

0 1 2 3 4 5

7: We have a process for each element of our business. They are simply illustrated and everyone sticks to them.

0 1 2 3 4 5

8: All the people in our organisation are the right people for our culture, sharing our core values.

0 1 2 3 4 5

9: Our organisation chart of roles, responsibilities and accountability is clear, constantly updated and understood by all.

0 1 2 3 4 5

10: Everyone is in the right job, performing the right role for their abilities and in flow at least 75% of their day

0 1 2 3 4 5

11: Our leadership team is open and honest. We have the right people in the right jobs.

0 1 2 3 4 5

12: Everyone has 90 day projects and are focused on them

0 1 2 3 4 5

13: Everyone has weekly laser focused milestone meetings with their teams.

0 1 2 3 4 5

14: All meetings have a clear agenda, start on time and end on time. The meeting leader understands the profile of each member in the group and relates to them accordingly.

0 1 2 3 4 5

15: All teams identify, discuss, and solve key issues for the greater good of the company and our clients, not individual benefit.

0 1 2 3 4 5

16: Our systems and procedures are simply documented, understood, and followed by all.

0 1 2 3 4 5

17: We have a system for receiving regular customer and employee feedback, and we know their level of satisfaction.

0 1 2 3 4 5

18: A dashboard for weekly performance metrics is in place and reported as KSI's (key success indicators).

0 1 2 3 4 5

19: Everyone in the business has a clear understanding of the sales process and their impact upon it.

0 1 2 3 4 5

20: We have a budget and are monitoring it regularly.

0 1 2 3 4 5

Your score ________/ 100

Eureka moments in the second E of EUREKA

* **Susanne's tips for running your marathon**
* **Cancun can help**
* **WTF**
* **Listen to your inner coach or the inner critic**
* **Where your focus goes, your energy flows**
* **September 30th Steve's birthday (don't forget)**
* **What are you aiming for, where are you heading?**
* **Do you use a sat nav?**
* **Hire attitude, teach skills**
* **Get your MOT - moment of truth**

So the second E in EUREKA was all about setting your goals clearly and about the long game.

How did you score on the MOT? This will provide some clear direction on things to fix to aid your business growth. Get in touch if you'd like some help with anything.

Next - let's look at K in the EUREKA - Killer questions

Chapter 6

EUREKA

Killer questions

***'The quality of your life is determined by the quality of your questions.'* Tony Robbins.**

For an audio series that I produced called *Success Leaves Clues* I interviewed leading figures in the personal development and coaching world. At one such interview with Peter Thomson, (a leading authority on productising your business as a speaker, trainer, coach or consultant) I recalled this Tony Robbins quote.

"I don't mean to criticise the great man, as what he says is true," explained Peter, "but I would add to it. I would also say this: The quality of your life is determined by the quality of your questions and having the good sense to listen and act upon the answers you receive."

Wise words from Tony and truly enhanced by Peter.

Ask great questions, listen, then act.

Remember **this is not a sales manual from the 80's**. I'm not about to offer you the top 10 killer questions to close more deals or the top 10 killer questions to ask at an interview. Instead, let's look at some killer questions you should be asking of yourself. Killer questions that will help create and embed your own 'yes' culture.

The subconscious mind is phenomenally complex, yet it makes no distinction between disruptive and constructive thought patterns. If you fill your head with negativity, fear, doubt, and disbelief in your ability to succeed, your subconscious mind will go to work to deliver the outcome for you. Conversely, feed your mind with positive thoughts and bingo! You get what you concentrate on.

Test this theory and you will find it applies to winners in most circles whether they are from business, sports, politics or the entertainment industry and it can work for you too.

I found the following verse in Napoleon Hill's bestselling book, *Think and Grow Rich*. It resonated with me so much as I typed it out I pinned it on the wall above my desk years ago; you might want to do the same. I found it a simple and effective way to regain focus and to rebuild my self-belief on days that I found particularly challenging.

The book was originally written in 1937. These are his words so please excuse what could be considered political incorrectness today by his references to *man* at the exclusion of *woman*.

If you think you're beaten, you are.
If you think you dare not, you don't.
If you like to win, but think you can't,
It's almost certain you won't.

If you think you'll lose, you're lost,
For out of this world we find,
Success begins with a fellows will,
It's all in a state of mind.

If you think you're outclassed, you are,
You've got to think height to rise,
You got to be sure of yourself,
Before you can ever win the prize.

Life's battles don't always go
To the stronger or faster man,
But sooner or later, the man who wins,
Is the man who thinks he can!

Those words certainly still strike a chord with me, how about you?

Other killer questions for you: Who do you hang out with? What kind of company do you keep? Do the people around you fuel you up or sap your energy?

As you read each line of the verse above can you see someone in your mind's eye who fits the bill?

If you think you're beaten you are.

We all know people like that, right? No matter how good things might be there's always the 'glass half empty' crew on hand ready to drag you down and smash your dreams. The eternal pessimists. The mood hoovers.

It's the closing line to the verse that always rings in my ears:

But sooner or later, the man who wins
Is the man who thinks he can!

That's all about positivity and self-belief; it's being optimistic and confident in your own abilities to succeed.

Winston Churchill summed it up beautifully this way:

'A pessimist sees the difficulty in every opportunity. An optimist sees the opportunity in every difficulty.'

We all know people that no matter how good things are they can only see the doom and gloom in any given situation. You shouldn't walk away from those people, you should RUN!

If that negative person happens to be your partner, husband or wife, don't get me wrong, I'm not advocating divorce or separation. I'm just suggesting you need to be mixing with people who will fuel your enthusiasm and help you achieve your goals, people that fit within a 'yes' culture.

Where are your optimists? What does your support network look like? Do you have a coach or mentor you can turn to? Think about it, there's not a single sportsperson you could name who doesn't have the coach or even a team of coaches to help keep them on track to achieve their goals. Why should you be any different?

.....

Don't go it alone

I act as a coach and mentor for a number of clients in various industries and yet I too, have coaches I turn to for help, who lift me up when I feel down. Mentors who help me get unstuck when I become stuck. They're capable of asking soul-searching, difficult questions that we avoid asking ourselves.

I also run a number of mentoring groups. Each month, positive, upbeat and enthusiastic business owners and senior managers meet to work 'on' their businesses not in them.

This is my kind of MBA: Mastermind, Brainstorm, Action.

The group act like a virtual board of directors, holding each other to account and asking questions of one another, the kind of killer questions that dig deep and get results. Find yourself a coach and mentor or a mentoring group.

Month on month the members of my mentoring programs are consistently achieving incredible results. Here's some of their feedback to give you food for thought. What results could you see from belonging to such a group? There's no need to battle things out alone.

'I was inspired to sign up to Steve's platinum coaching group after hearing him speak at a conference. In the 4 years working with Steve, he has more than delivered. Not just in marketing and sales though, although our 24 year old business has seen record sales months, but Steve has given me much more than that.

He has got me more focused on what makes me happy and how my business can help to deliver in these terms. What is the point of running your own business if you are just a slave to it? He has helped me cut through what I need to do and what I don't need to do.

Making me ask myself key questions has had a huge impact. I am less stressed, happier and have a clear way forward. I'm living the 'yes' culture.'

Gavin Rebello - Optometrist and entrepreneur.

'Constructive, direct, challenging yet supportive.

Steve and the group build mutual trust by really understanding who you are and your untapped potential and then, collaboratively, you put plans in place. Steve and the group hold you to task to achieve your goals.'

James Prior - Flying Start Ltd

'All thanks to you and the group, the deep searching questions, the quality of the speakers and the topics covered, our sales doubled again last month!

I can't thank you enough for helping me get to where we are today.'

Mark McIvor - Print Force Ltd

'Monthly meetings give you a wake up call as to why we're in business in the first place. We saw 150% increase in sales for the first 3 months.'

Howard Grahame - HG Education

'A key ingredient to the success of Platinum is the chemistry and quality of the people in the room and the killer questions we ask of ourselves every month.'

Amanda Johnson - VA Coaching and Training

'Steve and his group have literally transformed the way I think and act in business, our profits have soared since I became a member.'

Gary White - CBHC Accounting

'With the support and knowledge provided by the Platinum group, I have experienced tremendous personal and professional growth whilst faced with extremely challenging commercial pressures.'

Robert Sinnott - Acme Transport Services

'We doubled our sales last month and we're on for another cracker. The staff are 100% happier and far more efficient now they're in FLOW thanks to what we learn at Platinum.'

Tracy Ewen - Print Force Ltd.

'We were stuck in a bit of a rut... felt we needed something new to take us to the next level, Platinum has definitely delivered, now it's - how do we manage this torrential influx of work! And you're all helping with that too!'

Patricia Fox - Aralia Landscape and Garden Design

Lastly, one I'm particularly proud to be able to include.

He's been a member of one of my groups for over 4 years since starting his new business; here's a short comment from him to end on.

'Investing 5% of my time to work on my business for 146% increase in sales... Platinum works! Month in month out I'm hitting record months and my business is growing successfully.'

Matthew Day - CRM Superstars

Love it! It's this kind of feedback that fires me up each day. This is what my retirement is all about!

If you'd like information about my mentoring programs and to see how membership could help you. Email me to arrange a FREE chemistry call:

steve@steveclarke.info

(There's no automatic rite of passage based on payment, it's vital the chemistry of the groups is maintained, we can usually determine the suitability of the program for you and vice versa in a half hour conversation).

.....

Tough decision to make? Try to use your BRAINS.

Not entirely sure of the source or accuracy of this story, but let's agree to get over that for now!

My recollection is that the acronym (BRAINS) was originally credited in midwifery, feel free to confirm or point me in another direction, but for now let's get over that.

I've used this little acronym as a framework to help numerous clients wrestle with some major decisions over recent months to great effect and so thought I'd share it here with you.

Here are some killer questions for you to use the next time you have a tough decision to make – try using your **BRAINS**:

Benefit – list the benefits for you or your company or those for your client or prospect. Ask yourself what are the benefits of the product or service you are considering. Don't over analyse at this stage, just list them all and keep writing until you grind to a halt. Then review.

Risk – what could or would be put at risk by your decision one way or the other?

Alternatives – what are alternative actions you could take or products you could use or purchase? Here you could use the questions polygon from the Endurance chapter - Why, Who, When, Where and How?

Instinct – again don't over analyse. What is your gut feeling? What do your instincts tell you?

Nothing – what are the implications if you decide to simply do nothing?

Smile – having worked your challenge through this simple yet effective decision making process, whatever you decide, smile knowing you've made a decision and move on.
I can imagine this being used by a midwife, can you? What I know is it's a great structure to get you asking powerful killer questions. Try it out with the next decision you have to make or use it with your team.

.....

We must be mindful of our internal voices: who are you listening to, the coach or the critic? Whatever questions we ask ourselves our subconscious mind goes to work on it in order to deliver you the answer.

When things don't go to plan and you find yourself asking 'why me, why does this always happen to me?' Your subconscious dives into the filing cabinet and pulls out all the answers it can find to tell you why: you're useless, you always mess up or you're not worthy.

Instead you need to get into the habit of asking yourself different questions when the wheels fall off. Phrasing your questions differently will help you find the right solution.

What elements actually went well?

What could I do 5 % better next time?

How could I improve this and have fun at the same time?

Who could offer help and support?

Who might know the answer?

A member of my mentoring program, Juliet Price, MD of Park City Consulting, shared the following simple, yet highly effective, tool with the group. It can be used immediately after a meeting, a phone call, sales call or interview. I now have numerous clients who have built it into their staff appraisals.

www.ebi

Don't stick that into your browser - I take no responsibility for whatever website pops up!

In this instance it stands for:

What's Working Well… Even Better If.

You can see how this immediately focuses attention on the positive. What's working well?

No matter how small, you'll find things that went well.

You arrived on time and beat the traffic. You got the appointment in the first place. You presented yourself well at the interview, then it sends you off to look for improvements.

Was there a different person you should have met with? Should you have sent a proposal in advance? Should you have rehearsed your pitch more and tested assumptions?

Ask great questions, listen, then act.

'When you talk, you are only repeating what you already know. But if you listen, you may learn something new.' **Dalai Llama**

When I speak at conferences on sales and business growth topics, I will often start by asking the audience a question:

"By a quick show of hands, who in the room wants more clients and more sales?"

All the hands shoot into the air. (Particularly if a sales person is sitting with their boss). Then comes a moment of confusion that also gets their attention from the start.

"If you raised your hand, well that was the wrong answer."

"OK, to be fair, it was probably the wrong question. Let me ask the question slightly differently and see if you can recognise the difference."

I then pause as they settle and concentrate.

“Who here would like to attract more of the right kind of clients, that are a dream to work with, and that allow you to make an honest profit?”

Again all the hands shoot into the air, but this time with a big smile and often a cheer too as the penny drops.

Too many businesses spend time effort and energy on attracting the wrong kind of clients and even employees their way.

Can you see how the killer question has changed in such a way that your focus will be on attracting the right client as opposed to anyone that shows a vague interest?

If you have too many tyre kickers and time wasters who nickel and dime you on every deal, ask yourself and your teams: ‘How can we attract more of the right kind of clients, that are a dream to work with, and that allow you to make an honest profit?’

Even so, that’s still not the most effective killer question to ask if you want to create a ‘yes’ culture and live a ‘yes’ kind of a life. Your focus must be on building trust and adding value to others, not just thinking, what’s in it for you?

Give and you shall…? We all know the answer.

So the kind of questions you should be asking today to stand you apart from the crowd and to serve people better are:

How can I build trust?

How and where can I add value?

This applies at home, in relationships, in a new job, with your employees and with clients. Is this all making sense?

Take a moment now and make some notes. Ask yourself those questions in various areas of your life, then you've guessed it, listen to the answers and take action.

How can I build trust? And how and where can I add value?

Personal life… husband, wife, partner, kids, friends

Work… co-workers, bosses, clients, prospects

Eureka moments in the K of EUREKA

* **The quality of your life is determined by the quality of your questions**

* **Don't go it alone**

* **Tough decisions - use your BRAINS**

* **www.ebi**

* **How can I build trust?**

* **Where can I add value?**

Remember the quality of your life is determined by the quality of your questions and having the good sense to listen to the answers and then act upon them!

This leads us to A the final letter of the EUREKA acronym and final chapter of the book. Creating and embedding a 'yes' culture all comes down to your Attitude and the Actions you take.

It's your action that gets you traction.

Chapter 7

EUREKA

Attitude and Action

'It's your attitude, not your aptitude, that will determine your altitude.'
Zig Ziglar

I'm a firm believer that as Zig suggested many years ago, it's your attitude that will determine the altitude that you reach.

I mentioned in the opening chapter how a young Ford Cortina driver changed the course of my life by giving me a cassette tape. On the tape Zig Ziglar stated 'If you want to see a change it's down to you.' That was all about attitude and action.

Within hours of listening to that tape, I was ready to make some changes. I began scouring the local newspapers for potential job opportunities in sales and applying for the positions.

My CV was somewhat less than impressive. I was only 18, I lacked any qualifications and I also lacked the dreaded experience. As a result, back came the inevitable stream of replies: thanks, but no thanks. I know what it's like to face rejection. I knew it wasn't possible, but I actually felt I was getting more rejections than jobs I was applying for!

It was highly disheartening. My inner critics were suggesting maybe petrol pump attending was all I was fit for. Maybe I was destined to a life in greasy overalls. It's what I deserved for not working hard enough at school, but thankfully, Mr Ziglar's words echoed in my head. 'If you want to see a change, it's down to you.'

I began asking myself better questions. Why do I want to see a change? What could change? Who could help me? How could they help me? Although I didn't know it at the time I was running the Questions Pentagon. Asking myself the who, what, why questions backwards and forwards until I could find the answers.

Careers guidance for me at school was all but non-existent. In fact I remember the one occasion I was called in to meet our schools careers guidance officer.

"Come in Clarke, sit down."

"Thank you sir."

“So Clarke, what do you want to be when you leave school?”

“Rich and successful sir,” I replied in a very cocky, but honest way. Probably more cocky than honest, to be honest.

“I'm not going to waste my time if you can’t be serious get out. Next!” he snarled.

And that was it, careers guidance over.

.....

Church and welfare?

It was at that point my Dad stepped up. He offered to take me to a leading private vocational guidance centre on London's Harley Street. At its time this would have been at the very forefront of psychometric profiling.

After I completed the lengthy questionnaire it was the job of Professor Henderson to interpret and type up a full report. Keep in mind this predates computers so when I say type, I mean type on a manual typewriter!

The report, complete with accompanying graphs and charts, clearly indicated I was meant to be in sales. It delivered scores for personality, interests and aptitude.

For aptitude, the report actually scored me highest under a heading of ‘church and welfare’. What? On my initial reading I thought it was suggesting I study theology and become a vicar. It transpired when explained by Professor Henderson, that a high score under ‘church and welfare’ just indicated that whatever I was going to sell had to be of true benefit and add great value the buyer. i.e. not ice to the Eskimos, or sand to the Arabs - they've got enough in each case.

Armed with this report it was time for a different approach on the job application front.

Instead of sending a bland CV which could easily get lost in a sea of sameness, or dismissed through its lack of content and substance, I could send something other applicants would not be sending. The recommendation from Professor Henderson from a Harley Street clinic that I would be the right applicant for the sales position in question.

It worked like a dream. I stood out from the crowd and was finally invited for interviews.

There was no doubt that in each case the interviewers appreciated that I had gone the extra mile and taken action to demonstrate my suitability as a candidate. I attended three interviews in one week and received three job offers. I was about to begin my career in sales and leave the petrol pumps for good.

Recently, to my absolute delight, my Dad found the original report produced by Professor Henderson, way back when I was only 18. It's pretty scratchy, but check this out.

Off the charts for teaching, guidance and selling! But look at the next part.

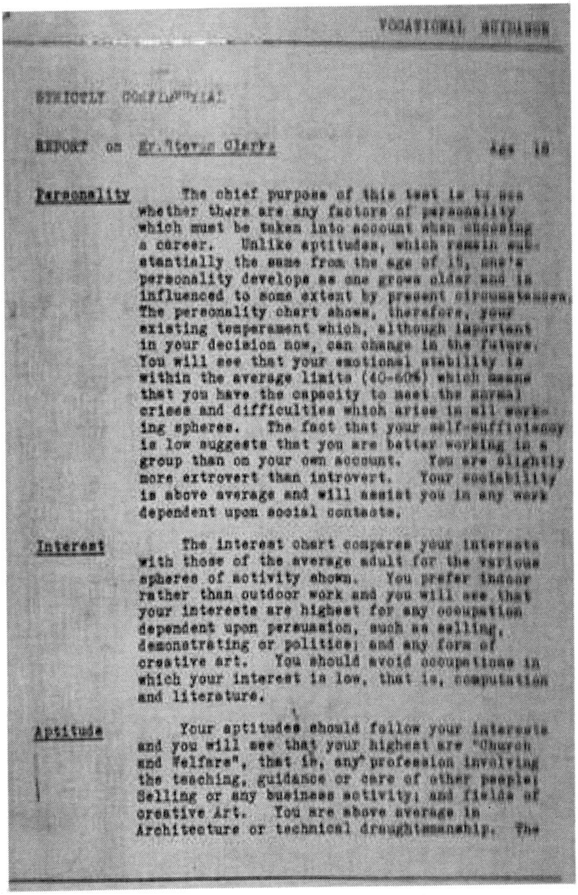

VOCATIONAL GUIDANCE

STRICTLY CONFIDENTIAL

REPORT on Mr. Steven Clarke Age 18

Personality The chief purpose of this test is to see whether there are any factors of personality which must be taken into account when choosing a career. Unlike aptitudes, which remain substantially the same from the age of 15, one's personality develops as one grows older and is influenced to some extent by present circumstances. The personality chart shows, therefore, your existing temperament which, although important in your decision now, can change in the future. You will see that your emotional stability is within the average limits (40-60%) which means that you have the capacity to meet the normal crises and difficulties which arise in all working spheres. The fact that your self-sufficiency is low suggests that you are better working in a group than on your own account. You are slightly more extrovert than introvert. Your sociability is above average and will assist you in any work dependent upon social contacts.

Interest The interest chart compares your interests with those of the average adult for the various spheres of activity shown. You prefer indoor rather than outdoor work and you will see that your interests are highest for any occupation dependent upon persuasion, such as selling, demonstrating or politics; and any form of creative art. You should avoid occupations in which your interest is low, that is, computation and literature.

Aptitude Your aptitudes should follow your interests and you will see that your highest are "Church and Welfare", that is, any profession involving the teaching, guidance or care of other people; Selling or any business activity; and fields of creative Art. You are above average in Architecture or technical draughtsmanship. The

At 18 he was signposting me to where I am today! 'Advising people on what they want into practical terms'.

Spooky stuff eh? Professor Henderson or Mystic Meg?

those of the average adult for the various spheres of activity shown. You prefer indoor rather than outdoor work and you will see that your interests are highest for any occupation dependent upon persuasion, such as selling, demonstrating or politics; and any form of creative art. You should avoid occupations in which your interest is low, that is, computation and literature.

Your aptitudes should follow your interests and you will see that your highest are "Church and Welfare", that is, any profession involving the teaching, guidance or care of other people; Selling or any business activity; and fields of creative Art. You are above average in Architecture or technical draughtsmanship. The

... using as an ... textiles you will
Straightaway you should find that you have a 'feeling' for them; you will talk easily and expressively to a potential customer about them. You will be disposed to help the client; you will make a sale - and a future 'return' customer.

You are, in our view, a first-class salesman of anything pertaining to textiles and furniture; you can be, equally, a <u>buyer</u> for a company, as well as a <u>seller</u>. But you can go further. You can be an independent adviser, with your own business - advising people on how to interpret what they want into practical terms.

If you want to get some practical experience of selling in the retail trade, then write to:

The Retail Distributors' Association,
Palladium House, 1 Argyll Street,
London, W1V 2LN.

asking for a list of Retail Distributors. Write to each Personnel Director, asking for an inter-

.....

Maybe it's time for an MBA.

In the early 1990s, (wow, last century, that makes me feel old), I started a winter sports business in the United States. It was initially self-funded, then as the reality of the mammoth task at hand sunk in, we raised much-needed additional capital through private angel investment to fund product development and take our product to market.

Three years later, in order to provide an exit for our investors, we completed an IPO (initial public offering), floating the company on the NASDAQ exchange.

Not too shabby for a former petrol pump attendant with no qualifications. It was all about attitude and action.

Remember the last verse from Napoleon Hill.

Life's battles don't always go
To the stronger or faster man,
But sooner or later, the man who wins
Is the man who thinks he can!

All we need to add is 'and takes action!'

Having floated my business on the stock market, it gave me the chance to think what I should do next. I had always been rather hung up over my lack of qualifications. Maybe now it was time to invest in my own education, perhaps I should complete an MBA I thought. I began looking into what was involved and what I could expect to achieve as a result of it. My hat goes off to anybody who has gone through the process!

To say it was complicated and involved would be a massive understatement. I concluded that by the end of an extremely arduous process I would be qualified and better equipped to do what I'd just done: start a company, grow a company and successfully exit a company. So what was the point in that?

But I really was hung up on my lack of qualifications. Somehow, I needed to prove to myself if nobody else, that I could learn, retain and utilise information. I really wanted a piece of paper to prove it, a certificate of some sort.

So instead of an MBA I decided to learn to fly a plane.

This meant I was actually going to have to take some written exams. It involved very real and practical exam elements too. You definitely need to know what you're doing when you're all on your own and there's 5000 feet of fresh air between your backside and planet Earth. It created plenty of WTF moments... Where's The Focus, and the other variety too!

There was a lot of classwork and studying to be done as well as the challenging practical side. My main challenge on the practical side was my fear of flying and fear of heights generally. (So maybe an MBA would have been a better choice you're thinking).

In some of my early self-development reading material I remember coming across an acronym for fear which you may well be familiar with.

False
Expectations
Appearing
Real

When I thought about it, my fear of flying, like most people with the same challenge, is not actually a fear of flying at all, it's a fear of crashing. I would be flying a single-engine, four seater, Piper Cherokee Warrior, PA 128. I didn't know anyone that had crashed one. So actually I was basing my fear on false expectations and making them appear real to the point that I feared them. Crazy.

I decided I should apply one of the following instead:

Fear
Everything
And
Run

Face
Everything
And
Rise

I chose the latter and went on to gain my private pilot's licence.

At the time we were living in the San Francisco Bay area. It was always great fun when friends from the UK would come to visit. I'd offer to take them on the ultimate sight- seeing trip around the bay out over the Golden Gate Bridge and buzzing Alcatraz, but I wouldn't tell them I'd actually be their pilot. So when they settled into the rear seats and I got in the front, closed the door and began playing with the instruments saying things like…

'I wonder what this switch does? It can't be that tough to fly one of these things, let's give it a bash!' Well, at least I found it amusing, I can't say that the passengers did at first!

The fine line between confidence and arrogance

As a student you have to learn a lot of theory about airframes and engines. One thing you discover is about the attitude of the aeroplane's wing in its relationship to the ground and how that will determine the altitude the plane will reach and how quickly it can rise.

It made me realise how similar this is to business and in life generally. As Zig Ziglar said 'It's your attitude that determines your altitude.'

I know so many people in life who will never reach the altitude they would like to and nine times out of ten it's because of their attitude and their limiting beliefs.

I can't tell you how many times a business owner has said to me 'I just can't seem to get off the ground, or this is a long hard slog, I don't seem to be getting to where I need to go fast enough.' Well that's just like flying.

Imagine you're sitting in your airplane ready for takeoff. If you sit at the end of the runway, put on half the power and you make a halfway commitment to a take off, what's going to happen? As you take the brakes off and start rolling down the runway on half throttle, how the hell do you think that plane is going to get in the air? With that attitude what's going to happen when you reach the end of the runway? You are just going to crash and burn. Same in business, same in your career, same in a relationship. Half throttle is no good. To reach new heights you need to change the attitude of the wing and give it full power.

So in business, I meet people who are ready to get going. They have their first business cards printed, their website almost up and running and they're off to their first networking event. They go and meet with people to try and find prospects and they charge down their metaphorical runway. Just as they get off the ground, they think 'Whoah! This is too scary, I don't like it,' and they try to drop their plane back on the ground. If they're lucky they have some runway left and will survive to give it another shot. Sadly many crash and burn on their first takeoff never to attempt to fly again.

Next time they commit to take off, they start to gain altitude, but slowly. This is when I hear people tell me it's taking so long to get to where we want to go. To gain altitude in your aeroplane and in business you need to continue your activity and inputs changing the attitude of the wing and increasing power. You have to respond and react to information on the instruments in the cockpit, weather conditions, and other air traffic around you. That's how you will increase your altitude.

It's the same in business. Once you're off the ground you've got more marketing to do, more phone calls to make, more meetings to attend, more proposals to write. It can sometimes seem never-ending. The more you do and the more focus you maintain the greater the results.

In aviation terms, Vx is the indicated forward airspeed for best angle of climb. This is the largest angle the aircraft can climb at without overloading and stalling the wing. The most efficient rate of a steady climb.

Do you want a steady climb? Do you aspire to mediocrity? Do you want to go at the same rate of climb as the masses? If that's what you want, that's perfectly fine, but don't beat yourself up at not reaching new heights.

If you want to reach the highest altitude possible, you might need to climb steeper and put in more power, you'll need to adjust the attitude of your wing again, but exercise caution.

Often when people start to fly high or achieve great results very quickly they can become arrogant. Nobody likes arrogant people. They start to lose the support of people around them and very quickly performance and attitudes can begin to nosedive.

In an aeroplane, if you become overly arrogant and climb too steeply above Vx you lose the support of something very important, it's called 'lift'. An alarm will sound in the cockpit to warn the pilot that he or she is about to stall. If the alarm is ignored and the controls aren't altered, the wing stalls, you lose lift, the right wing tips over and the nose drops down. The plane begins an often uncontrollable spiral dive towards the ground.

In order to achieve the altitude you wish to reach you must maintain the right attitude. There is often quite a fine line between confidence and arrogance, be sure you don't cross the line.

.....

Don't be a crap magnet

I have a 7 day challenge for you. Are you up for it? It's very much related to your attitude and action.

Why do some people succeed where others fail? It's a big question, but I firmly believe there aren't too many answers.

All the successful people I know have made a decision to create the life and the business they want. The rest, many of them great people, so don't get me wrong, take what comes their way, they just drift from day to day, they accept that things just happen to them.

But here's what I see. The doers, the achievers, the people I see having extraordinary success in their lives and their businesses take control. They are in the driver's seat, they have the steering wheel firmly in hand, they take control, responsibility and they take action!

What of the others? They take the role of the 'victim.' There are always reasons why things don't come their way, why they don't get the orders, why the cash flows, but always the wrong way. Why they don't get selected for interviews, can't find the right partner and so on.

Here are three things I have observed from people that say they want to succeed in business and in life, but often, why they fail to meet their goals.

Blame. They will always find someone or something to blame on the lack of sales, lack of profits or lack of success. They'll blame the government, the economy, their competitors, anyone but themselves.

Justify. They will usually attempt to justify that things are ok. They'll say things like…

'Well, it's not all about the money; it's not that important'.

Take that attitude and it won't be with you for long if ever at all. Imagine saying the same about your husband or wife, they'll not be around for long either!

Complain. Complainers attract crap like a magnet! Sorry, but it's true. It's proven time and time again that you attract what you focus on. Complain and moan about everything and things will only get worse.

When I deliver keynote talks I often give the audience a challenge. I'd like to offer you the same challenge right here, right now. Are you ready?

For the next seven days. No complaining.

Will you take the challenge? I think you'll be blown away with the changes it can deliver. Go on. I dare you!

Consider this, we are creatures of habit, right? Yet we're not born with the habits, we learn them. Monkey see, monkey do. We've all heard that, well we're not so far removed from the monkey, are we? We learn our responses to circumstances and situations, so it figures we can learn different patterns too and not just take what comes our way.

Just like robots, we get programmed a particular way, with certain patterns and behaviours. You can paint the robot so it looks great, looks new, but the programming is just the same and so the results will be too.

What stops people from achieving the level of success of others and changing their programming, their beliefs and behaviour to reach new heights? Fear. Fear of the unknown, fear of failure, fear of uncertainty.

Are successful people fearless? No, not at all, but they take action in spite of fear!

Nike took three words to get their message across, I will say it in just two – DO IT. Take the seven day no complaining challenge - it can change your world.

We are controlled by our thoughts which produce feelings, our feelings translate into action and the action we take delivers results. Simple.

If your thoughts of business growth or success fill you with fear and dread, feelings of potential failure or uncertainty and doubt, how powerful do you suppose the actions you take will be? *Feel the fear and do it anyway*, (the title of a great book by Susan Jeffers). You don't need to look at the results you're getting now as the best results you can achieve. Instead, consider your results as the fruit on a tree. You can't change the fruit once it's there, that's too late.

If you want to see change, if you want different results look to the roots, that's where you need to make changes. That's why we call it the root cause. Cause and effect. Change the roots and you can change the effect; the fruits and the results.

What are you going to focus on and think about? Good stuff or bad, problems or solutions? What you focus on is what you'll feel. How you feel will determine the action you will take and the results you'll get – the fruit on your tree.

Once you take decisive action in pursuit of your goals, the fear melts away and confidence grows.

Now stop complaining, let's see the results you want and deserve. It worked for me and it can work for you too.

.....

Dessert could be back on the menu for you too

My wife and I have been married a good long while, we have 5 kids between us. We've had our share of stressful times with teenagers, challenging school days, endless ferrying of them to sports and dance classes, boyfriend issues, (with the girls, not my wife). Plenty to complain about. Often we were just ships that seemed to pass in the night. We are truly blessed to have five wonderful children between us. They have all now grown-up and moved away from home. I feel truly blessed!

If you happen to be a parent of teenage children you will understand and appreciate that teenagers quite literally speak another language, in fact sometimes they seem like they're from a different planet. They come with challenges, maybe they should come with a health warning! Teenagers grow up. I couldn't be more proud of every one of our children and what beautiful adults they turned into.

We've both had businesses to run and a home to manage at the same time too. We've hit the wall as we all do with the classic work life balance stuff. There's always loads we can complain about.

But let me tell you when Mr Grumpy comes home from work, moaning and groaning about everything, guess what's? There's no 'dessert' on the menu for him and that's more to complain about. It's a vicious circle if you're not careful.

When you learn to stop complaining there are numerous benefits. Not least of which is that when Mr Happy comes home in the evening instead of Mr Grumpy and guess what? Dessert is back on the menu, metaphorically speaking!

Take the 7 day no complaining challenge, it will change your world. The rules are simple:

You need to achieve at least seven consecutive days without complaining to gain the full effect. So if on day one you find yourself complaining about the traffic on the way to work, that's OK. Stop the clock and reset.

If on day three you slip into a rant about a canceled order or one of the children not doing their homework again, that's OK. Stop the clock, reset. Yes! It has to be seven consecutive days. Go for it. You have nothing to lose and everything to gain.

.....

For action - Get chunky - Give me a break!

Chunky is good? Yep, let me explain how you can get more done in your day than you ever thought possible. Here's a question for you. What's one common denominator you can think of across all of mankind? What do all human beings have in common? You can probably think of a few things if you put your mind to it.

Here's one to consider. Irrespective of your age, sex, colour or creed, irrespective of your social standing, the job you do or anything else we all have just 24 hours in a day. We are all given the same time just 1,440 minutes in each day.

So how is it some people get so much more done in their day than others? I've always been fascinated by this. It turns out there's a science behind it.

What do you do that leaves you feeling drained, stressed and believing there's never enough time in the day to get stuff done. What is it that all too often creates this sense of overwhelm and frustration? Does this strike a chord with you? If not you it will with people that work for you or with you so please read on.

Do you work as well with your clients or colleagues consistently throughout the day? Do you think as creatively or clearly or produce a consistent quality of work all thought the day, or have you noticed peaks and troughs?

This is because we, as human beings we aren't wired to operate like computers. We all have these ups and downs in our day, it's normal.

The question is how could understanding and harnessing this knowledge massively boost your productivity and production as well as satisfaction and sustainability? That would be good to know, wouldn't it?

Here's what I've discovered.

Over 50 years ago, a leading pioneer in sleep research, a Russian by the name of Nathaniel Kleitman, discovered something he called the "basic rest-activity cycle" – the 90 minute periods at night during which we move progressively through five stages of sleep, from light to deep, and then out again. You may have heard of REM sleep – Rapid Eye

Movement Sleep, this is what I'm referring to – periods of deep rejuvenating sleep.

Although it may be less well known, Kleitman also noticed that our bodies operate by the same 90 minute rhythm during the day. When we're awake, the movement is from higher to lower alertness. This is called our 'ultradian performance rhythm'.

When we need a rest, our bodies sends us clear signals such as fatigue, hunger, drowsiness, and loss of focus and the fidgets. But mostly, we override them, drink coffee, eat chocolate or energy bars and plough on regardless.

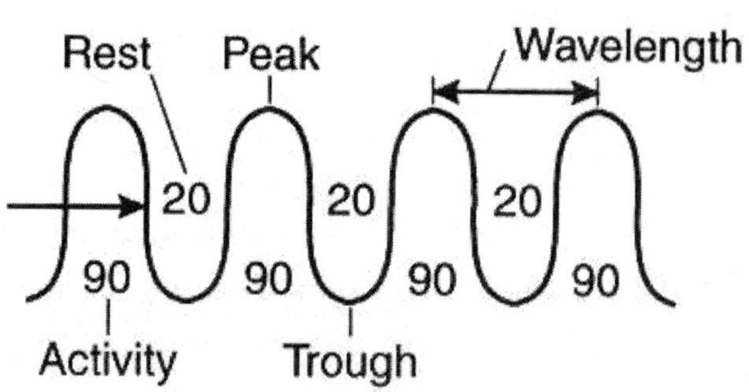

Ultradian Rhythm

There's a better way – a far more effective way to get more done and not feel stressed.

Get 'chunky'.

By this I mean – work in 90 minute chunks, then rest for 20 minutes and repeat. You might remember it best like this 'Work at the peak, rest in the valley'.

If you're looking for growth in your business or have a task to complete, commit to what I call a 'Power Hour Plus'. Not all day. Just select your 90 consecutive minutes and commit to working on your project and nothing else in that solid 90 minutes – your Power Hour Plus.

Find the best time of day that suits you. Create the right environment. Switch off phones and don't even think about looking at email or Facebook! You are uninterruptible by anyone for any reason for 90 minutes!

For me it's usually 6.00 am – 7.30 am. During that time I commit my time and energy solely to focused business growth work. Working on my business not in it. Activity that will get new clients or keep existing ones happy. No distractions, no excuses.

This is one secret successful people in business apply consistently to get more productive time in their day and to achieve incredible results – you can too. Try this for a month, 90 minutes a day; create a new habit. The results are excellent.

'We are what we repeatedly do. Excellence then is not an act, but a habit.' **Aristotle.**

.....

Action is effortless when you're in Flow

Imagine a river as it winds its way down a hillside effortlessly gathering speed as it flows over rocks and boulders making its way to sea. It's almost unstoppable, it's relentless, it's only going in one direction towards the sea and nothing is going to stop it. It's totally in flow.

Have you ever had a day when you felt like that?

Unstoppable, totally in flow. A day when you get your head down and crack on with a task and the next time you look up it's already lunch time. You think to yourself, where has the time gone? That's you in Flow. Doing what you enjoy, probably doing what you're naturally best at.

Put simply, Flow is the path of least resistance. When you are in a team in Flow, productivity increases, results improve dramatically, you have more fun and feel more connected to the organisation.

All too often we have tasks thrust upon us or simply can't see who that job could be delegated to and so we take it on. These tasks will take longer than necessary and cause frustration and anxiety in the wrong hands. It's like swimming up stream in a fast running river, not going with the flow.

For me I'm in flow when I'm presenting, delivering a talk or running a seminar. I'm outgoing, people orientated and quite creative. I'm a starter, not a completer. I'm absolutely not a detail person. Facts, figures, spread sheets and data... arrrggghhh they drive me to distraction.

For other people this is their natural default position. Cold hard facts. Don't paint me pictures, give me the data; speak in public? I'd rather stick pins in my eyes!

We're all quite different. So it makes sense to me that we should learn to play to our strengths and not try to strengthen our weaknesses.

This will be my last acronym of the book. I promise.

What does DOA stand for?

Dead On Arrival, is the answer most people give me. For me, it stands for Delegate, Outsource, Automate.

When you understand your unique profile and where you are most naturally in flow, you will find it much easier to delegate to another team member whose profile is better suited to the task, you could outsource it, or automate it.

Make a list now of all of the 'stuff' you have to attend to during your normal working day. This is an honesty moment. Nobody else needs to see this. How do you actually spend your time? You don't have to do this from memory. Actually take time to note down how you spend your time during the day as you do it.

Now take a moment to think about a typical working day for you. What percentage of your day would you say you are 'in flow'? Doing what you love, doing what fires you up, doing what energises you? Doing what you're best at and when you're being really productive? How about an average week and month?

7.00 __________

7.30 __________

8.00 __________

8.30 __________

9.00 __________

9.30 __________

10.00 __________

10.30 __________

11.00 __________

11.30 __________

12.00 __________

12.30 __________

13.00 __________

13.30 __________

14.00 __________

14.30 __________

15.00 __________

15.30 ____

16.00 ____

16.30 ____

17.00 ____

17.30 ____

18.00 ____

18.30 ____

OK - that'll do!

I'm in flow __________ % of my day

I'm in flow __________ % of my week

I'm in flow __________ % of my month

.....

Talent Dynamics

I made reference earlier in the book to a psychometric profile system I use called Talent Dynamics, it's incredible.

You may be familiar with other systems such as Myers Briggs and DISC. For me Talent Dynamics beats them all. It just makes so much sense, it's easy to understand and easy to apply.

In business Talent Dynamics works because it delivers results in performance and profitability while aligning your team to the spirit and purpose at the heart of your organisation.

Based on an ancient Chinese philosophy and given a modern twist, Talent Dynamics allows each person in a team or organisation to understand the quickest and easiest way for them to get into and stay in Flow. It helps them understand how to get others into and staying in Flow and provides clear strategies and actions for teams to take based on their profile, to achieve a desired result.

Which profile are you and what does it mean?

There are a number of ways I could help you improve your productivity or that of your teams using Talent Dynamics profiling.

It could be used to help you get your ideal job, don't forget it was a very early psychometric profile test by Professor Henderson from the Harley Street Clinic that helped me get on the first rung of my career ladder many years ago. This could help you too!

Talent Dynamics profile and debrief

If you want to go deeper and get even more insights about how your profile can be used to add more value to your business or company so that you achieve more results with less stress, get paid at a high level and have more fun in the process take this test! Wherever you are in the world you can take the test on-line.

This powerful, but quick and easy to complete on-line test, assesses your strengths, productivity, values and behaviour in order to determine which one of the 8 Talent Dynamic Profiles you are. From this we can help you identify your "flow" state and show you how to spend more time in it, so you add more value to your business or company.

You'll have a focused 45 minute follow up coaching session via Skype with one of our top Talent Dynamic Flow Consultants who will help you unlock your true potential, release you from your frustrations and focus you on breakthrough strategies you'll want to implement in your business and life as they are based on your specific results.

We only have room for a limited number of these each month so book your session now!

Email steve@steveclarke.info for info today.

Talent Dynamics Team Acceleration

Most businesses and companies are not harnessing anywhere close to the true potential in their people and this loss of passion and productivity costs millions.

But now there is a way to not just stop it, but to turn it around by tapping into the true talents of each and every person on your team, no matter how big or small your team or business is. The Talent Dynamics Team Acceleration day harnesses the profiles of your team mixed with expert facilitation and coaching from one of our team to create a true Business Development Pathway for Accelerating Trust, Flow and Growth.

Imagine a team that worked well together, could anticipate each other and could back each other up. A team fully 'in flow.' What economic impact would that have on your business or organisation?

Email steve@steveclarke.info for info today.

Talent Dynamics for Sales

Recruiting, managing and running a sales team of any size is a very challenging role for an entrepreneur, sales manager or even sales director, especially if you don't know the Talent Dynamic Profiles of your sales people!

Without this insight how will you know which part of the team they are best suited to so that they can add the most value to win the business? The Regular, Reluctant or Referral?

Should they be involved in new business or in growing and developing existing accounts? How do you keep such different personalities motivated and performing at their peak? All these questions and more are not only answered but clearly mapped out which is guaranteed to double your team's performance, increase sales and productivity. The world of selling has changed forever - have you and your teams?

Email steve@steveclarke.info today for info.

Eureka moments in the A of EUREKA

* Your attitude determines your altitude

* Church and welfare

* Maybe it' s time for an MBA

* The fine line between confidence and arrogance

* Don't be a crap magnet

* Dessert could be back on the menu

* For action - get chunky

* Action is effortless when you're in flow

* Talent dynamic

So that's it. 'EUREKA Moments! Creating a 'yes' culture' in your life and in your business ultimately comes down to six key ingredients:

Engagement
Uncovering the pain
Rapport and reach
Endurance
Killer questions
Attitude and Action

Take action today!

...And they all lived happily ever after...

(I was struggling to finish writing this book. I'm a starter not a completer or finisher. In frustration I posted a plea for help and support on Facebook. Facebook gives you reach.

William Tallis from Pearly Grey Resort in Tenerife suggested 'And they all lived happily ever after'. I liked that, so used it. The truth is, when you create a 'yes' culture, it's a happy state to be in.

The same post also resulted in me securing an editor, designer, proof reader and publisher for the book. Thanks Andy Gibney of 3P Publishing!

About the author

Steve Clarke - Inspirational Business Growth Speaker.

He has taken his own businesses from start up to stock market flotation. Another to a successful multi-million pound sale and exit.

He walks his talk. Everything he shares is from practical first hand experience and not hollow theory.

Steve has an obvious and instant affinity with entrepreneurial business owners of small to medium size businesses, so a perfect fit for a mixed business audience.

He's equally at home with corporates, large sales teams and professional services.

Not just another sales trainer who speaks; he has unique material and poignant personal stories to share that will help everyone within an organisation understand that today sales isn't someone's job, it's everyone's job.

His belief is that every business, from a one man or one woman band to a multinational giant has three distinct sales teams to consider, The Regular, The Reluctant and The Referral. He provides effective strategies for each that will drop straight to your bottom line.

What Steve has to share on the subjects of sales, marketing and customer service can deliver transformational and lasting change to any organisation that embraces and embeds his methodology.

He leaves an audience feeling fully engaged and inspired whatever their role in the business.

Steve has been privileged to speak to audiences all around the globe, across 5 continents. The same questions cross every industry sector, geographical and cultural boundary.

How can we generate more leads, increase sales and profits? How can we recruit motivate and keep the right team members? That's precisely where he can help. It's what makes his subject matter relevant, Steve makes it interesting and memorable.

To find out about Steve's availability to speak at your event and discover how he can help you.

Call: +44 7946 227082

Visit www.steveclarke.info

Email: steve@steveclarke.info

"*I heard Steve deliver a series of outstanding leadership talks in Lithuania. I immediately hired him to address our company and to mentor our leadership team for two years, helping us grow from $150m to over $300m in annual revenues.*"
Gui Peres
Head of Global Sales, Ergomotion Inc. USA

"*I attended Steve Customer Service masterclass in Malta. It was fantastic. I implemented one simple change to one element of our service and secured a major new client as a result.*"
Stefania Calleja
General Manager, The Food Company, Malta

"*Steve is the master of the conversational keynote. His unique style gets his points across in a way that is highly accessible and actionable for the audience. Laughing and learning go hand in hand when he speaks*"
Gordon Tredgold, CEO Leadership

"We've engaged a wide range in national and international speakers, but none more powerful and relevant in today's competitive market than Steve.
Motivational, inspirational, mesmerising, and down to earth were repeat comments from delegates. Steve really does tick all the boxes. Can't recommend him highly enough as a conference speaker."
Paul Surridge
CEO, Sight Care Group

"I wanted a world class speaker to open our seminar in Spain and I got one – truly amazing!.
Steve has passion and humour. He really cares that the audience leave with actionable ideas and techniques. I cannot recommend him highly enough, he's definitely top of my list of great speakers."
Gina Marks
Managing Director, GM Events